CW00482518

A FIRST WORLD WAR POETRY COLLECTION

THE GREATEST WARTIME POEMS OF THE FIRST WORLD WAR'S MOST BELOVED WAR POETS

RUPERT BROOKE   JOHN MCCRAE   WILFRED OWEN

ALAN SEEGER

———

CONTENTS

1914 & OTHER POEMS BY RUPERT BROOKE

WAR POEMS BY WILFRED OWEN

IN FLANDERS FIELDS & OTHER POEMS BY JOHN MCCRAE

1914 & OTHER POEMS BY RUPERT BROOKE

1914

I. PEACE

Now, God be thanked Who has matched us with His
    hour,
And caught our youth, and wakened us from sleeping,
With hand made sure, clear eye, and sharpened power,
To turn, as swimmers into cleanness leaping,
Glad from a world grown old and cold and weary,
Leave the sick hearts that honour could not move,
And half-men, and their dirty songs and dreary,
And all the little emptiness of love!

Oh! we, who have known shame, we have found release
    there,
Where there's no ill, no grief, but sleep has mending,
Naught broken save this body, lost but breath;
Nothing to shake the laughing heart's long peace there
But only agony, and that has ending;
And the worst friend and enemy is but Death.

II. SAFETY

Dear! of all happy in the hour, most blest
He who has found our hid security,
Assured in the dark tides of the world that rest,
And heard our word, 'Who is so safe as we?'
We have found safety with all things undying,
The winds, and morning, tears of men and mirth,
The deep night, and birds singing, and clouds flying,
And sleep, and freedom, and the autumnal earth.
We have built a house that is not for Time's throwing.
We have gained a peace unshaken by pain for ever.
War knows no power. Safe shall be my going,
Secretly armed against all death's endeavour;
Safe though all safety's lost; safe where men fall;
And if these poor limbs die, safest of all.

III. THE DEAD

Blow out, you bugles, over the rich Dead!
There's none of these so lonely and poor of old,
But, dying, has made us rarer gifts than gold.
These laid the world away; poured out the red
Sweet wine of youth; gave up the years to be
Of work and joy, and that unhoped serene,
That men call age; and those who would have been,
Their sons, they gave, their immortality.

Blow, bugles, blow! They brought us, for our dearth,
Holiness, lacked so long, and Love, and Pain.
Honour has come back, as a king, to earth,
And paid his subjects with a royal wage;
And Nobleness walks in our ways again;
And we have come into our heritage.

IV. THE DEAD

These hearts were woven of human joys and cares,

Washed marvellously with sorrow, swift to mirth.
The years had given them kindness. Dawn was theirs,
And sunset, and the colours of the earth.
These had seen movement, and heard music; known
Slumber and waking; loved; gone proudly friended;
Felt the quick stir of wonder; sat alone;
Touched flowers and furs and cheeks. All this is ended.

There are waters blown by changing winds to laughter
And lit by the rich skies, all day. And after,
Frost, with a gesture, stays the waves that dance
And wandering loveliness. He leaves a white
Unbroken glory, a gathered radiance,
A width, a shining peace, under the night.

V. THE SOLDIER

If I should die, think only this of me:
That there's some corner of a foreign field
That is for ever England. There shall be
In that rich earth a richer dust concealed;
A dust whom England bore, shaped, made aware,
Gave, once, her flowers to love, her ways to roam,
A body of England's, breathing English air,
Washed by the rivers, blest by suns of home.

And think, this heart, all evil shed away,
A pulse in the eternal mind, no less
Gives somewhere back the thoughts by England given;
Her sights and sounds; dreams happy as her day;
And laughter, learnt of friends; and gentleness,
In hearts at peace, under an English heaven.

THE TREASURE

When colour goes home into the eyes,
And lights that shine are shut again
With dancing girls and sweet birds' cries

Behind the gateways of the brain;
And that no-place which gave them birth, shall close
The rainbow and the rose:—

Still may Time hold some golden space
Where I'll unpack that scented store
Of song and flower and sky and face,
And count, and touch, and turn them o'er,
Musing upon them; as a mother, who
Has watched her children all the rich day through
Sits, quiet-handed, in the fading light,
When children sleep, ere night.

THE SOUTH SEAS

TIARE TAHITI

Mamua, when our laughter ends,
And hearts and bodies, brown as white,
Are dust about the doors of friends,
Or scent ablowing down the night,
Then, oh! then, the wise agree,
Comes our immortality.
Mamua, there waits a land
Hard for us to understand.
Out of time, beyond the sun,
All are one in Paradise,
You and Pupure are one,
And Taü, and the ungainly wise.
There the Eternals are, and there
The Good, the Lovely, and the True,
And Types, whose earthly copies were
The foolish broken things we knew;
There is the Face, whose ghosts we are;
The real, the never-setting Star;
And the Flower, of which we love
Faint and fading shadows here;
Never a tear, but only Grief;
Dance, but not the limbs that move;

Songs in Song shall disappear;
Instead of lovers, Love shall be;
For hearts, Immutability;
And there, on the Ideal Reef,
Thunders the Everlasting Sea!

And my laughter, and my pain,
Shall home to the Eternal Brain.
And all lovely things, they say,
Meet in Loveliness again;
Miri's laugh, Teïpo's feet,
And the hands of Matua,
Stars and sunlight there shall meet,
Coral's hues and rainbows there,
And Teüra's braided hair;
And with the starred *tiare's* white,
And white birds in the dark ravine,
And *flamboyants* ablaze at night,
And jewels, and evening's after-green,
And dawns of pearl and gold and red,
Mamua, your lovelier head!
And there'll no more be one who dreams
Under the ferns, of crumbling stuff,
Eyes of illusion, mouth that seems,
All time-entangled human love.
And you'll no longer swing and sway
Divinely down the scented shade,
Where feet to Ambulation fade,
And moons are lost in endless Day.
How shall we wind these wreaths of ours,
Where there are neither heads nor flowers?
Oh, Heaven's Heaven!—but we'll be missing
The palms, and sunlight, and the south;
And there's an end, I think, of kissing,
When our mouths are one with Mouth....

Taü here, Mamua,
Crown the hair, and come away!
Hear the calling of the moon,

And the whispering scents that stray
About the idle warm lagoon.
Hasten, hand in human hand,
Down the dark, the flowered way,
Along the whiteness of the sand,
And in the water's soft caress,
Wash the mind of foolishness,
Mamua, until the day.
Spend the glittering moonlight there
Pursuing down the soundless deep
Limbs that gleam and shadowy hair,
Or floating lazy, half-asleep.
Dive and double and follow after,
Snare in flowers, and kiss, and call,
With lips that fade, and human laughter
And faces individual,
Well this side of Paradise!...
There's little comfort in the wise.

PAPEETE, *February* 1914

RETROSPECT

In your arms was still delight,
Quiet as a street at night;
And thoughts of you, I do remember,
Were green leaves in a darkened chamber,
Were dark clouds in a moonless sky.
Love, in you, went passing by,
Penetrative, remote, and rare,
Like a bird in the wide air,
And, as the bird, it left no trace
In the heaven of your face.
In your stupidity I found
The sweet hush after a sweet sound.
All about you was the light
That dims the greying end of night;
Desire was the unrisen sun,
Joy the day not yet begun,

9

With tree whispering to tree,
Without wind, quietly.
Wisdom slept within your hair,
And Long-Suffering was there,
And, in the flowing of your dress,
Undiscerning Tenderness.
And when you thought, it seemed to me,
Infinitely, and like a sea,
About the slight world you had known
Your vast unconsciousness was thrown....

O haven without wave or tide!
Silence, in which all songs have died!
Holy book, where hearts are still!
And home at length under the hill!
O mother quiet, breasts of peace,
Where love itself would faint and cease!
O infinite deep I never knew,
I would come back, come back to you,
Find you, as a pool unstirred,
Kneel down by you, and never a word,
Lay my head, and nothing said,
In your hands, ungarlanded;
And a long watch you would keep;
And I should sleep, and I should sleep!

MATAIEA, *January* 1914

THE GREAT LOVER

I have been so great a lover: filled my days
So proudly with the splendour of Love's praise,
The pain, the calm, and the astonishment,
Desire illimitable, and still content,
And all dear names men use, to cheat despair,
For the perplexed and viewless streams that bear
Our hearts at random down the dark of life.
Now, ere the unthinking silence on that strife
Steals down, I would cheat drowsy Death so far,

My night shall be remembered for a star
That outshone all the suns of all men's days.
Shall I not crown them with immortal praise
Whom I have loved, who have given me, dared with me
High secrets, and in darkness knelt to see
The inenarrable godhead of delight?
Love is a flame;—we have beaconed the world's night.
A city:—and we have built it, these and I.
An emperor:—we have taught the world to die.
So, for their sakes I loved, ere I go hence,
And the high cause of Love's magnificence,
And to keep loyalties young, I'll write those names
Golden for ever, eagles, crying flames,
And set them as a banner, that men may know,
To dare the generations, burn, and blow
Out on the wind of Time, shining and streaming....
These I have loved:

            White plates and cups, clean-gleaming,
Ringed with blue lines; and feathery, faery dust;
Wet roofs, beneath the lamp-light; the strong crust
Of friendly bread; and many-tasting food;
Rainbows; and the blue bitter smoke of wood;
And radiant raindrops couching in cool flowers;
And flowers themselves, that sway through sunny hours,
Dreaming of moths that drink them under the moon;
Then, the cool kindliness of sheets, that soon
Smooth away trouble; and the rough male kiss
Of blankets; grainy wood; live hair that is
Shining and free; blue-massing clouds; the keen
Unpassioned beauty of a great machine;
The benison of hot water; furs to touch;
The good smell of old clothes; and other such—
The comfortable smell of friendly fingers,
Hair's fragrance, and the musty reek that lingers
About dead leaves and last year's ferns....

                    Dear names,
And thousand other throng to me! Royal flames;
Sweet water's dimpling laugh from tap or spring;
Holes in the ground; and voices that do sing;
Voices in laughter, too; and body's pain,
Soon turned to peace; and the deep-panting train;
Firm sands; the little dulling edge of foam
That browns and dwindles as the wave goes home;
And washen stones, gay for an hour; the cold
Graveness of iron; moist black earthen mould;
Sleep; and high places; footprints in the dew;
And oaks; and brown horse-chestnuts, glossy-new;
And new-peeled sticks; and shining pools on grass;—
All these have been my loves. And these shall pass,
Whatever passes not, in the great hour,
Nor all my passion, all my prayers, have power
To hold them with me through the gate of Death.
They'll play deserter, turn with the traitor breath,
Break the high bond we made, and sell Love's trust
And sacramented covenant to the dust.
—Oh, never a doubt but, somewhere, I shall wake,
And give what's left of love again, and make
New friends, now strangers....

                    But the best I've known,
Stays here, and changes, breaks, grows old, is blown
About the winds of the world, and fades from brains
Of living men, and dies.
                    Nothing remains.

O dear my loves, O faithless, once again
This one last gift I give: that after men
Shall know, and later lovers, far-removed,
Praise you, "All these were lovely"; say, "He loved."

MATAIEA, 1914

HEAVEN

Fish (fly-replete, in depth of June,
Dawdling away their wat'ry noon)
Ponder deep wisdom, dark or clear,
Each secret fishy hope or fear.
Fish say, they have their Stream and Pond;
But is there anything Beyond?
This life cannot be All, they swear,
For how unpleasant, if it were!
One may not doubt that, somehow, Good
Shall come of Water and of Mud;
And, sure, the reverent eye must see
A Purpose in Liquidity.
We darkly know, by Faith we cry,
The future is not Wholly Dry.
Mud unto mud!—Death eddies near—
Not here the appointed End, not here!
But somewhere, beyond Space and Time,
Is wetter water, slimier slime!
And there (they trust) there swimmeth One
Who swam ere rivers were begun,
Immense, of fishy form and mind,
Squamous, omnipotent, and kind;
And under that Almighty Fin,
The littlest fish may enter in.
Oh! never fly conceals a hook,
Fish say, in the Eternal Brook,
But more than mundane weeds are there,
And mud, celestially fair;
Fat caterpillars drift around,
And Paradisal grubs are found;
Unfading moths, immortal flies,
And the worm that never dies.
And in that Heaven of all their wish,
There shall be no more land, say fish.

DOUBTS

When she sleeps, her soul, I know,
Goes a wanderer on the air,
Wings where I may never go,
Leaves her lying, still and fair,
Waiting, empty, laid aside,
Like a dress upon a chair....
This I know, and yet I know
Doubts that will not be denied.

For if the soul be not in place,
What has laid trouble in her face?
And, sits there nothing ware and wise
Behind the curtains of her eyes,
What is it, in the self's eclipse,
Shadows, soft and passingly,
About the corners of her lips,
The smile that is essential she?

And if the spirit be not there,
Why is fragrance in the hair?

THERE'S WISDOM IN WOMEN

"Oh love is fair, and love is rare;" my dear one she said,
"But love goes lightly over." I bowed her foolish head,
And kissed her hair and laughed at her. Such a child
    was she;
So new to love, so true to love, and she spoke so bitterly.

But there's wisdom in women, of more than they have
    known,
And thoughts go blowing through them, are wiser than
    their own,
Or how should my dear one, being ignorant and young,
Have cried on love so bitterly, with so true a tongue?

HE WONDERS WHETHER TO PRAISE OR TO BLAME HER

I have peace to weigh your worth, now all is over,
But if to praise or blame you, cannot say.
For, who decries the loved, decries the lover;
Yet what man lauds the thing he's thrown away?

Be you, in truth, this dull, slight, cloudy naught,
The more fool I, so great a fool to adore;
But if you're that high goddess once I thought,
The more your godhead is, I lose the more.

Dear fool, pity the fool who thought you clever!
Dear wisdom, do not mock the fool that missed you!
Most fair,—the blind has lost your face for ever!
Most foul,—how could I see you while I kissed you?

So ... the poor love of fools and blind I've proved you,
For, foul or lovely, 'twas a fool that loved you.

A MEMORY (FROM A SONNET-SEQUENCE)

Somewhile before the dawn I rose, and stept
Softly along the dim way to your room,
And found you sleeping in the quiet gloom,
And holiness about you as you slept.
I knelt there; till your waking fingers crept
About my head, and held it. I had rest
Unhoped this side of Heaven, beneath your breast.
I knelt a long time, still; nor even wept.

It was great wrong you did me; and for gain
Of that poor moment's kindliness, and ease,
And sleepy mother-comfort!
                Child, you know
How easily love leaps out to dreams like these,
Who has seen them true. And love that's wakened so

Takes all too long to lay asleep again.

ONE DAY

Today I have been happy. All the day
I held the memory of you, and wove
Its laughter with the dancing light o' the spray,
And sowed the sky with tiny clouds of love,
And sent you following the white waves of sea,
And crowned your head with fancies, nothing worth,
Stray buds from that old dust of misery,
Being glad with a new foolish quiet mirth.

So lightly I played with those dark memories,
Just as a child, beneath the summer skies,
Plays hour by hour with a strange shining stone,
For which (he knows not) towns were fire of old,
And love has been betrayed, and murder done,
And great kings turned to a little bitter mould.

THE PACIFIC, OCTOBER 1913

WAIKIKI

Warm perfumes like a breath from vine and tree
Drift down the darkness. Plangent, hidden from eyes,
Somewhere an *eukaleli* thrills and cries
And stabs with pain the night's brown savagery.
And dark scents whisper; and dim waves creep to me,
Gleam like a woman's hair, stretch out, and rise;
And new stars burn into the ancient skies,
Over the murmurous soft Hawaian sea.

And I recall, lose, grasp, forget again,
And still remember, a tale I have heard, or known
An empty tale, of idleness and pain,

Of two that loved—or did not love—and one
Whose perplexed heart did evil, foolishly,
A long while since, and by some other sea.

WAIKIKI, 1913

HAUNTINGS

In the grey tumult of these after years
Oft silence falls; the incessant wranglers part;
And less-than-echoes of remembered tears
Hush all the loud confusion of the heart;
And a shade, through the toss'd ranks of mirth and
     crying
Hungers, and pains, and each dull passionate mood,—
Quite lost, and all but all forgot, undying,
Comes back the ecstasy of your quietude.

So a poor ghost, beside his misty streams,
Is haunted by strange doubts, evasive dreams,
Hints of a pre-Lethean life, of men,
Stars, rocks, and flesh, things unintelligible,
And light on waving grass, he knows not when,
And feet that ran, but where, he cannot tell.

THE PACIFIC, 1914

SONNET (SUGGESTED BY SOME OF THE PROCEEDINGS
OF THE SOCIETY FOR PSYCHICAL RESEARCH)

Not with vain tears, when we're beyond the sun,
We'll beat on the substantial doors, nor tread
Those dusty high-roads of the aimless dead
Plaintive for Earth; but rather turn and run
Down some close-covered by-way of the air,
Some low sweet alley between wind and wind,
Stoop under faint gleams, thread the shadows, find
Some whispering ghost-forgotten nook, and there

Spend in pure converse our eternal day;
Think each in each, immediately wise;
Learn all we lacked before; hear, know, and say
What this tumultuous body now denies;
And feel, who have laid our groping hands away;
And see, no longer blinded by our eyes.

CLOUDS

Down the blue night the unending columns press
In noiseless tumult, break and wave and flow,
Now tread the far South, or lift rounds of snow
Up to the white moon's hidden loveliness.
Some pause in their grave wandering comradeless,
And turn with profound gesture vague and slow,
As who would pray good for the world, but know
Their benediction empty as they bless.

They say that the Dead die not, but remain
Near to the rich heirs of their grief and mirth.
I think they ride the calm mid-heaven, as these,
In wise majestic melancholy train,
And watch the moon, and the still-raging seas,
And men, coming and going on the earth.

THE PACIFIC, *OCTOBER* 1913

MUTABILITY

They say there's a high windless world and strange,
Out of the wash of days and temporal tide,
Where Faith and Good, Wisdom and Truth abide,
Æterna corpora, subject to no change.
There the sure suns of these pale shadows move;
There stand the immortal ensigns of our war;
Our melting flesh fixed Beauty there, a star,
And perishing hearts, imperishable Love....

18

Dear, we know only that we sigh, kiss, smile;
Each kiss lasts but the kissing; and grief goes over;
Love has no habitation but the heart.
Poor straws! on the dark flood we catch awhile,
Cling, and are borne into the night apart.
The laugh dies with the lips, 'Love' with the lover.

SOUTH KENSINGTON—MAKAWELI, 1913

THE BUSY HEART

Now that we've done our best and worst, and parted,
I would fill my mind with thoughts that will not rend.
(O heart, I do not dare go empty-hearted)
I'll think of Love in books, Love without end;
Women with child, content; and old men sleeping;
And wet strong ploughlands, scarred for certain grain;
And babes that weep, and so forget their weeping;
And the young heavens, forgetful after rain;
And evening hush, broken by homing wings;
And Song's nobility, and Wisdom holy,
That live, we dead. I would think of a thousand things,
Lovely and durable, and taste them slowly,
One after one, like tasting a sweet food.
I have need to busy my heart with quietude.

LOVE

Love is a breach in the walls, a broken gate,
Where that comes in that shall not go again;
Love sells the proud heart's citadel to Fate.
They have known shame, who love unloved. Even then,

When two mouths, thirsty each for each, find slaking,
And agony's forgot, and hushed the crying
Of credulous hearts, in heaven—such are but taking
Their own poor dreams within their arms, and lying
Each in his lonely night, each with a ghost.
Some share that night. But they know, love grows colder,
Grows false and dull, that was sweet lies at most.
Astonishment is no more in hand or shoulder,
But darkens, and dies out from kiss to kiss.
All this is love; and all love is but this.

UNFORTUNATE

Heart, you are restless as a paper scrap
That's tossed down dusty pavements by the wind;
Saying, "She is most wise, patient and kind.
Between the small hands folded in her lap
Surely a shamed head may bow down at length,
And find forgiveness where the shadows stir
About her lips, and wisdom in her strength,
Peace in her peace. Come to her, come to her!"...

She will not care. She'll smile to see me come,
So that I think all Heaven in flower to fold me.
She'll give me all I ask, kiss me and hold me,
And open wide upon that holy air
The gates of peace, and take my tiredness home,
Kinder than God. But, heart, she will not care.

THE CHILTERNS

Your hands, my dear, adorable,
Your lips of tenderness
—Oh, I've loved you faithfully and well,
Three years, or a bit less.
It wasn't a success.

Thank God, that's done! and I'll take the road,
Quit of my youth and you,
The Roman road to Wendover
By Tring and Lilley Hoo,
As a free man may do.

For youth goes over, the joys that fly,
The tears that follow fast;
And the dirtiest things we do must lie
Forgotten at the last;
Even Love goes past.

What's left behind I shall not find,
The splendour and the pain;
The splash of sun, the shouting wind,
And the brave sting of rain,
I may not meet again.

But the years, that take the best away,
Give something in the end;
And a better friend than love have they,
For none to mar or mend,
That have themselves to friend.

I shall desire and I shall find
The best of my desires;
The autumn road, the mellow wind
That soothes the darkening shires.
And laughter, and inn-fires.

White mist about the black hedgerows,
The slumbering Midland plain,
The silence where the clover grows,
And the dead leaves in the lane,
Certainly, these remain.

And I shall find some girl perhaps,
And a better one than you,
With eyes as wise, but kindlier,
And lips as soft, but true.
And I daresay she will do.

HOME

I came back late and tired last night
Into my little room,
To the long chair and the firelight
And comfortable gloom.

But as I entered softly in
I saw a woman there,
The line of neck and cheek and chin,
The darkness of her hair,
The form of one I did not know
Sitting in my chair.

I stood a moment fierce and still,
Watching her neck and hair.
I made a step to her; and saw
That there was no one there.

It was some trick of the firelight
That made me see her there.
It was a chance of shade and light
And the cushion in the chair.

Oh, all you happy over the earth,
That night, how could I sleep?
I lay and watched the lonely gloom;
And watched the moonlight creep
From wall to basin, round the room.
All night I could not sleep.

Hands and lit faces eddy to a line;
The dazed last minutes click; the clamour dies.
Beyond the great-swung arc o' the roof, divine,
Night, smoky-scarv'd, with thousand coloured eyes

Glares the imperious mystery of the way.
Thirsty for dark, you feel the long-limbed train
Throb, stretch, thrill motion, slide, pull out and sway,
Strain for the far, pause, draw to strength again....

As a man, caught by some great hour, will rise,
Slow-limbed, to meet the light or find his love;
And, breathing long, with staring sightless eyes,
Hands out, head back, agape and silent, move

Sure as a flood, smooth as a vast wind blowing;
And, gathering power and purpose as he goes,
Unstumbling, unreluctant, strong, unknowing,
Borne by a will not his, that lifts, that grows,

Sweep out to darkness, triumphing in his goal,
Out of the fire, out of the little room....
—There is an end appointed, O my soul!
Crimson and green the signals burn; the gloom

Is hung with steam's far-blowing livid streamers.
Lost into God, as lights in light, we fly,
Grown one with will, end-drunken huddled dreamers.
The white lights roar. The sounds of the world die.

And lips and laughter are forgotten things.
Speed sharpens; grows. Into the night, and on,
The strength and splendour of our purpose swings.
The lamps fade; and the stars. We are alone.

SONG

All suddenly the wind comes soft,
And Spring is here again;
And the hawthorn quickens with buds of green,
And my heart with buds of pain.

My heart all Winter lay so numb,
The earth so dead and frore,
That I never thought the Spring would come,
Or my heart wake any more.

But Winter's broken and earth has woken,
And the small birds cry again;
And the hawthorn hedge puts forth its buds,
And my heart puts forth its pain.

BEAUTY AND BEAUTY

When Beauty and Beauty meet
All naked, fair to fair,
The earth is crying-sweet,
And scattering-bright the air,
Eddying, dizzying, closing round,
With soft and drunken laughter;
Veiling all that may befall
After—after—

Where Beauty and Beauty met,
Earth's still a-tremble there,
And winds are scented yet,
And memory-soft the air,
Bosoming, folding glints of light,
And shreds of shadowy laughter;
Not the tears that fill the years
After—after—

THE WAY THAT LOVERS USE

The way that lovers use is this;
They bow, catch hands, with never a word,
And their lips meet, and they do kiss,
—So I have heard.

They queerly find some healing so,
And strange attainment in the touch;
There is a secret lovers know,
—I have read as much.

And theirs no longer joy nor smart,
Changing or ending, night or day;
But mouth to mouth, and heart on heart,
—So lovers say.

MARY AND GABRIEL

Young Mary, loitering once her garden way,
Felt a warm splendour grow in the April day,
As wine that blushes water through. And soon,
Out of the gold air of the afternoon,
One knelt before her: hair he had, or fire,
Bound back above his ears with golden wire,
Baring the eager marble of his face.
Not man's nor woman's was the immortal grace
Rounding the limbs beneath that robe of white,
And lighting the proud eyes with changeless light,
Incurious. Calm as his wings, and fair,
That presence filled the garden.
                                        She stood there,
Saying, "What would you, Sir?"
                                        He told his word,
"Blessed art thou of women!" Half she heard,
Hands folded and face bowed, half long had known,
The message of that clear and holy tone,
That fluttered hot sweet sobs about her heart;

Such serene tidings moved such human smart.
Her breath came quick as little flakes of snow.
Her hands crept up her breast. She did but know
It was not hers. She felt a trembling stir
Within her body, a will too strong for her
That held and filled and mastered all. With eyes
Closed, and a thousand soft short broken sighs,
She gave submission; fearful, meek, and glad....

She wished to speak. Under her breasts she had
Such multitudinous burnings, to and fro,
And throbs not understood; she did not know
If they were hurt or joy for her; but only
That she was grown strange to herself, half lonely,
All wonderful, filled full of pains to come
And thoughts she dare not think, swift thoughts and
    dumb,
Human, and quaint, her own, yet very far,
Divine, dear, terrible, familiar...
Her heart was faint for telling; to relate
Her limbs' sweet treachery, her strange high estate,
Over and over, whispering, half revealing,
Weeping; and so find kindness to her healing.
'Twixt tears and laughter, panic hurrying her,
She raised her eyes to that fair messenger.
He knelt unmoved, immortal; with his eyes
Gazing beyond her, calm to the calm skies;
Radiant, untroubled in his wisdom, kind.
His sheaf of lilies stirred not in the wind.
How should she, pitiful with mortality,
Try the wide peace of that felicity
With ripples of her perplexed shaken heart,
And hints of human ecstasy, human smart,
And whispers of the lonely weight she bore,
And how her womb within was hers no more
And at length hers?
                    Being tired, she bowed her head;
And said, "So be it!"
                    The great wings were spread

Showering glory on the fields, and fire.
The whole air, singing, bore him up, and higher,
Unswerving, unreluctant. Soon he shone
A gold speck in the gold skies; then was gone.

The air was colder, and grey. She stood alone.

THE FUNERAL OF YOUTH: THRENODY

The day that *Youth* had died,
There came to his grave-side,
In decent mourning, from the county's ends,
Those scatter'd friends
Who had lived the boon companions of his prime,
And laughed with him and sung with him and wasted,
In feast and wine and many-crown'd carouse,
The days and nights and dawnings of the time
When *Youth* kept open house,
Nor left untasted
Aught of his high emprise and ventures dear,
No quest of his unshar'd—
All these, with loitering feet and sad head bar'd,
Followed their old friend's bier.
Folly went first,
With muffled bells and coxcomb still revers'd;
And after trod the bearers, hat in hand—
Laughter, most hoarse, and Captain *Pride* with tanned
And martial face all grim, and fussy *Joy*,
Who had to catch a train, and *Lust*, poor, snivelling boy;
These bore the dear departed.
Behind them, broken-hearted,
Came *Grief*, so noisy a widow, that all said,
"Had he but wed
Her elder sister *Sorrow*, in her stead!"
And by her, trying to soothe her all the time,
The fatherless children, *Colour*, *Tune*, and *Rhyme*
(The sweet lad *Rhyme*), ran all-uncomprehending.
Then, at the way's sad ending,

29

Round the raw grave they stay'd. Old *Wisdom* read,
In mumbling tone, the Service for the Dead.
There stood *Romance*,
The furrowing tears had mark'd her rougèd cheek;
Poor old *Conceit*, his wonder unassuaged;
Dead *Innocency's* daughter, *Ignorance*;
And shabby, ill-dress'd *Generosity*;
And *Argument*, too full of woe to speak;
Passion, grown portly, something middle-aged;
And *Friendship*—not a minute older, she;
Impatience, ever taking out his watch;
Faith, who was deaf, and had to lean, to catch
Old *Wisdom's* endless drone.
Beauty was there,
Pale in her black; dry-eyed; she stood alone.
Poor maz'd *Imagination*; *Fancy* wild;
Ardour, the sunlight on his greying hair;
Contentment, who had known *Youth* as a child
And never seen him since. And *Spring* came too,
Dancing over the tombs, and brought him flowers—
She did not stay for long.
And *Truth*, and *Grace*, and all the merry crew,
The laughing *Winds* and *Rivers*, and lithe *Hours*;
And *Hope*, the dewy-eyed; and sorrowing *Song*;—
Yes, with much woe and mourning general,
At dead *Youth's* funeral,
Even these were met once more together, all,
Who erst the fair and living *Youth* did know;
All, except only *Love*. *Love* had died long ago.

THE OLD VICARAGE, GRANTCHESTER: (CAFÉ DES WESTENS, BERLIN, MAY 1912)

Just now the lilac is in bloom,
All before my little room;
And in my flower-beds, I think,
Smile the carnation and the pink;
And down the borders, well I know,
The poppy and the pansy blow...
Oh! there the chestnuts, summer through,
Beside the river make for you
A tunnel of green gloom, and sleep
Deeply above; and green and deep
The stream mysterious glides beneath,
Green as a dream and deep as death.
—Oh, damn! I know it! and I know
How the May fields all golden show,
And when the day is young and sweet,
Gild gloriously the bare feet
That run to bathe...
        Du lieber Gott!

Here am I, sweating, sick, and hot,
And there the shadowed waters fresh
Lean up to embrace the naked flesh.
Temperamentvoll German Jews
Drink beer around;—and *there* the dews
Are soft beneath a morn of gold,
Here tulips bloom as they are told;
Unkempt about those hedges blows
An English unofficial rose;
And there the unregulated sun
Slopes down to rest when day is done,
And wakes a vague unpunctual star,
A slippered Hesper; and there are
Meads towards Haslingfield and Coton
Where das *Betreten's* not *verboten.*

31

εἴθε γενοίμην... Would I were
In Grantchester, in Grantchester!—
Some, it may be, can get in touch
With Nature there, or Earth, or such.
And clever modern men have seen
A Faun a-peeping through the green,
And felt the Classics were not dead,
To glimpse a Naiad's reedy head,
Or hear the Goat-foot piping low:...
But these are things I do not know.
I only know that you may lie
Day long and watch the Cambridge sky,
And, flower-lulled in sleepy grass,
Hear the cool lapse of hours pass,
Until the centuries blend and blur
In Grantchester, in Grantchester....
Still in the dawnlit waters cool
His ghostly Lordship swims his pool,
And tries the strokes, essays the tricks,
Long learnt on Hellespont, or Styx.
Dan Chaucer hears his river still
Chatter beneath a phantom mill.
Tennyson notes, with studious eye,
How Cambridge waters hurry by...
And in that garden, black and white,
Creep whispers through the grass all night;
And spectral dance, before the dawn,
A hundred Vicars down the lawn;
Curates, long dust, will come and go
On lissom, clerical, printless toe;
And oft between the boughs is seen
The sly shade of a Rural Dean...
Till, at a shiver in the skies,
Vanishing with Satanic cries,
The prim ecclesiastic rout
Leaves but a startled sleeper-out,
Grey heavens, the first bird's drowsy calls,
The falling house that never falls.

God! I will pack, and take a train,
And get me to England once again!
For England's the one land, I know,
Where men with Splendid Hearts may go;
And Cambridgeshire, of all England,
The shire for Men who Understand;
And of *that* district I prefer
The lovely hamlet Grantchester.
For Cambridge people rarely smile,
Being urban, squat, and packed with guile;
And Royston men in the far South
Are black and fierce and strange of mouth;
At Over they fling oaths at one,
And worse than oaths at Trumpington,
And Ditton girls are mean and dirty,
And there's none in Harston under thirty,
And folks in Shelford and those parts
Have twisted lips and twisted hearts,
And Barton men make Cockney rhymes,
And Coton's full of nameless crimes,
And things are done you'd not believe
At Madingley, on Christmas Eve.
Strong men have run for miles and miles,
When one from Cherry Hinton smiles;
Strong men have blanched, and shot their wives,
Rather than send them to St. Ives;
Strong men have cried like babes, bydam,
To hear what happened at Babraham.
But Grantchester! ah, Grantchester!
There's peace and holy quiet there,
Great clouds along pacific skies,
And men and women with straight eyes,
Lithe children lovelier than a dream,
A bosky wood, a slumbrous stream,
And little kindly winds that creep
Round twilight corners, half asleep.
In Grantchester their skins are white;
They bathe by day, they bathe by night;
The women there do all they ought;

The men observe the Rules of Thought.
They love the Good; they worship Truth;
They laugh uproariously in youth;
(And when they get to feeling old,
They up and shoot themselves, I'm told)...

Ah God! to see the branches stir
Across the moon at Grantchester!
To smell the thrilling-sweet and rotten
Unforgettable, unforgotten
River-smell, and hear the breeze
Sobbing in the little trees.
Say, do the elm-clumps greatly stand
Still guardians of that holy land?
The chestnuts shade, in reverend dream,
The yet unacademic stream?
Is dawn a secret shy and cold
Anadyomene, silver-gold?
And sunset still a golden sea
From Haslingfield to Madingley?
And after, ere the night is born,
Do hares come out about the corn?
Oh, is the water sweet and cool,
Gentle and brown, above the pool?
And laughs the immortal river still
Under the mill, under the mill?
Say, is there Beauty yet to find?
And Certainty? and Quiet kind?
Deep meadows yet, for to forget
The lies, and truths, and pain?... oh! yet
Stands the Church clock at ten to three?
And is there honey still for tea?

WAR POEMS BY WILFRED OWEN

POEMS

PREFACE

THIS BOOK IS NOT about heroes. English Poetry is not yet fit to speak of them. Nor is it about deeds or lands, nor anything about glory, honour, dominion or power,

except War.
Above all, this book is not concerned with Poetry.
The subject of it is War, and the pity of War.
The Poetry is in the pity.
Yet these elegies are not to this generation,
      This is in no sense consolatory.

They may be to the next.
All the poet can do to-day is to warn.
That is why the true Poets must be truthful.
If I thought the letter of this book would last,
I might have used proper names; but if the spirit of it
      survives Prussia,—my ambition and those names will
      be content; for they will have achieved themselves
      fresher fields than Flanders.

Note.—This Preface was found, in an unfinished condition, among Wilfred Owen's papers.

37

STRANGE MEETING

It seemed that out of the battle I escaped
Down some profound dull tunnel, long since scooped
Through granites which Titanic wars had groined.
Yet also there encumbered sleepers groaned,
Too fast in thought or death to be bestirred.
Then, as I probed them, one sprang up, and stared
With piteous recognition in fixed eyes,
Lifting distressful hands as if to bless.
And by his smile, I knew that sullen hall;
With a thousand fears that vision's face was grained;
Yet no blood reached there from the upper ground,
And no guns thumped, or down the flues made moan.
"Strange, friend," I said, "Here is no cause to mourn."
"None," said the other, "Save the undone years,
The hopelessness. Whatever hope is yours,
Was my life also; I went hunting wild
After the wildest beauty in the world,
Which lies not calm in eyes, or braided hair,
But mocks the steady running of the hour,
And if it grieves, grieves richlier than here.
For by my glee might many men have laughed,
And of my weeping something has been left,
Which must die now. I mean the truth untold,
The pity of war, the pity war distilled.
Now men will go content with what we spoiled.
Or, discontent, boil bloody, and be spilled.
They will be swift with swiftness of the tigress,
None will break ranks, though nations trek from progress.
Courage was mine, and I had mystery;
Wisdom was mine, and I had mastery;
To miss the march of this retreating world
Into vain citadels that are not walled.
Then, when much blood had clogged their chariot-wheels
I would go up and wash them from sweet wells,
Even with truths that lie too deep for taint.
I would have poured my spirit without stint
But not through wounds; not on the cess of war.

Foreheads of men have bled where no wounds were.
I am the enemy you killed, my friend.
I knew you in this dark; for so you frowned
Yesterday through me as you jabbed and killed.
I parried; but my hands were loath and cold.
Let us sleep now . . ."

(This poem was found among the author's papers. It ends on this strange note.)

Another Version

Earth's wheels run oiled with blood. Forget we that.
Let us lie down and dig ourselves in thought.
Beauty is yours and you have mastery,
Wisdom is mine, and I have mystery.
We two will stay behind and keep our troth.
Let us forego men's minds that are brute's natures,
Let us not sup the blood which some say nurtures,
Be we not swift with swiftness of the tigress.
Let us break ranks from those who trek from progress.
Miss we the march of this retreating world
Into old citadels that are not walled.
Let us lie out and hold the open truth.
Then when their blood hath clogged the chariot wheels
We will go up and wash them from deep wells.
What though we sink from men as pitchers falling
Many shall raise us up to be their filling
Even from wells we sunk too deep for war
And filled by brows that bled where no wounds were.

Alternative line—

Even as One who bled where no wounds were.

GREATER LOVE

Red lips are not so red
As the stained stones kissed by the English dead.

39

Kindness of wooed and wooer
Seems shame to their love pure.
O Love, your eyes lose lure
When I behold eyes blinded in my stead!

Your slender attitude
Trembles not exquisite like limbs knife-skewed,
Rolling and rolling there
Where God seems not to care;
Till the fierce Love they bear
Cramps them in death's extreme decrepitude.

Your voice sings not so soft,—
Though even as wind murmuring through raftered loft,—
Your dear voice is not dear,
Gentle, and evening clear,
As theirs whom none now hear
Now earth has stopped their piteous mouths that
    coughed.

Heart, you were never hot,
Nor large, nor full like hearts made great with shot;
And though your hand be pale,
Paler are all which trail
Your cross through flame and hail:
Weep, you may weep, for you may touch them not.

APOLOGIA PRO POEMATE MEO

I, too, saw God through mud—
The mud that cracked on cheeks when wretches smiled.
War brought more glory to their eyes than blood,
And gave their laughs more glee than shakes a child.

Merry it was to laugh there—
Where death becomes absurd and life absurder.
For power was on us as we slashed bones bare
Not to feel sickness or remorse of murder.

I, too, have dropped off fear—
Behind the barrage, dead as my platoon,
And sailed my spirit surging, light and clear
Past the entanglement where hopes lay strewn;

And witnessed exultation—
Faces that used to curse me, scowl for scowl,
Shine and lift up with passion of oblation,
Seraphic for an hour; though they were foul.

I have made fellowships—
Untold of happy lovers in old song.
For love is not the binding of fair lips
With the soft silk of eyes that look and long,

By Joy, whose ribbon slips,—
But wound with war's hard wire whose stakes are strong;
Bound with the bandage of the arm that drips;
Knit in the welding of the rifle-thong.

I have perceived much beauty
In the hoarse oaths that kept our courage straight;
Heard music in the silentness of duty;
Found peace where shell-storms spouted reddest spate.

Nevertheless, except you share
With them in hell the sorrowful dark of hell,
Whose world is but the trembling of a flare,
And heaven but as the highway for a shell,

You shall not hear their mirth:
You shall not come to think them well content
By any jest of mine. These men are worth
Your tears: You are not worth their merriment.

November 1917.

THE SHOW

My soul looked down from a vague height with Death,
As unremembering how I rose or why,
And saw a sad land, weak with sweats of dearth,
Gray, cratered like the moon with hollow woe,
And fitted with great pocks and scabs of plaques.

Across its beard, that horror of harsh wire,
There moved thin caterpillars, slowly uncoiled.
It seemed they pushed themselves to be as plugs
Of ditches, where they writhed and shrivelled, killed.

By them had slimy paths been trailed and scraped
Round myriad warts that might be little hills.

From gloom's last dregs these long-strung creatures crept,
And vanished out of dawn down hidden holes.

(And smell came up from those foul openings
As out of mouths, or deep wounds deepening.)

On dithering feet upgathered, more and more,
Brown strings towards strings of gray, with bristling
        spines,
All migrants from green fields, intent on mire.

Those that were gray, of more abundant spawns,
Ramped on the rest and ate them and were eaten.

I saw their bitten backs curve, loop, and straighten,
I watched those agonies curl, lift, and flatten.

Whereat, in terror what that sight might mean,
I reeled and shivered earthward like a feather.

And Death fell with me, like a deepening moan.
And He, picking a manner of worm, which half had hid
Its bruises in the earth, but crawled no further,

Showed me its feet, the feet of many men,
And the fresh-severed head of it, my head.

MENTAL CASES

Who are these? Why sit they here in twilight?
Wherefore rock they, purgatorial shadows,
Drooping tongues from jaws that slob their relish,
Baring teeth that leer like skulls' tongues wicked?
Stroke on stroke of pain,—but what slow panic,
Gouged these chasms round their fretted sockets?
Ever from their hair and through their hand palms
Misery swelters. Surely we have perished
Sleeping, and walk hell; but who these hellish?

—These are men whose minds the Dead have ravished.
Memory fingers in their hair of murders,
Multitudinous murders they once witnessed.
Wading sloughs of flesh these helpless wander,
Treading blood from lungs that had loved laughter.
Always they must see these things and hear them,
Batter of guns and shatter of flying muscles,
Carnage incomparable and human squander
Rucked too thick for these men's extrication.

Therefore still their eyeballs shrink tormented
Back into their brains, because on their sense
Sunlight seems a bloodsmear; night comes blood-black;
Dawn breaks open like a wound that bleeds afresh
—Thus their heads wear this hilarious, hideous,
Awful falseness of set-smiling corpses.
—Thus their hands are plucking at each other;
Picking at the rope-knots of their scourging;
Snatching after us who smote them, brother,
Pawing us who dealt them war and madness.

PARABLE OF THE OLD MEN AND THE YOUNG

So Abram rose, and clave the wood, and went,
And took the fire with him, and a knife.
And as they sojourned both of them together,
Isaac the first-born spake and said, My Father,
Behold the preparations, fire and iron,
But where the lamb for this burnt-offering?
Then Abram bound the youth with belts and straps,
And builded parapets and trenches there,
And stretch\ed forth the knife to slay his son.
When lo! an angel called him out of heaven,
Saying, Lay not thy hand upon the lad,
Neither do anything to him. Behold,
A ram caught in a thicket by its horns;
Offer the Ram of Pride instead of him.
But the old man would not so, but slew his son. . . .

ARMS AND THE BOY

Let the boy try along this bayonet-blade
How cold steel is, and keen with hunger of blood;
Blue with all malice, like a madman's flash;
And thinly drawn with famishing for flesh.

Lend him to stroke these blind, blunt bullet-heads
Which long to muzzle in the hearts of lads.
Or give him cartridges of fine zinc teeth,
Sharp with the sharpness of grief and death.

For his teeth seem for laughing round an apple.
There lurk no claws behind his fingers supple;
And God will grow no talons at his heels,
Nor antlers through the thickness of his curls.

ANTHEM FOR DOOMED YOUTH

What passing-bells for these who die as cattle?

Only the monstrous anger of the guns.
Only the stuttering rifles' rapid rattle
Can patter out their hasty orisons.
No mockeries for them; no prayers nor bells,
Nor any voice of mourning save the choirs,—
The shrill, demented choirs of wailing shells;
And bugles calling for them from sad shires.

What candles may be held to speed them all?
Not in the hands of boys, but in their eyes
Shall shine the holy glimmers of goodbyes.
The pallor of girls' brows shall be their pall;
Their flowers the tenderness of patient minds,
And each slow dusk a drawing-down of blinds.

THE SEND-OFF

Down the close, darkening lanes they sang their way
To the siding-shed,
And lined the train with faces grimly gay.

Their breasts were stuck all white with wreath and spray
As men's are, dead.

Dull porters watched them, and a casual tramp
Stood staring hard,
Sorry to miss them from the upland camp.
Then, unmoved, signals nodded, and a lamp
Winked to the guard.

So secretly, like wrongs hushed-up, they went.
They were not ours:
We never heard to which front these were sent.

Nor there if they yet mock what women meant
Who gave them flowers.

Shall they return to beatings of great bells
In wild trainloads?

A few, a few, too few for drums and yells,
May creep back, silent, to still village wells
Up half-known roads.

INSENSIBILITY

I.

Happy are men who yet before they are killed
Can let their veins run cold.
Whom no compassion fleers
Or makes their feet
Sore on the alleys cobbled with their brothers.
The front line withers,
But they are troops who fade, not flowers
For poets' tearful fooling:
Men, gaps for filling
Losses who might have fought
Longer; but no one bothers.

II.

And some cease feeling
Even themselves or for themselves.
Dullness best solves
The tease and doubt of shelling,
And Chance's strange arithmetic
Comes simpler than the reckoning of their shilling.
They keep no check on Armies' decimation.

III.

Happy are these who lose imagination:
They have enough to carry with ammunition.
Their spirit drags no pack.
Their old wounds save with cold can not more ache.
Having seen all things red,
Their eyes are rid
Of the hurt of the colour of blood for ever.

And terror's first constriction over,
Their hearts remain small drawn.
Their senses in some scorching cautery of battle
Now long since ironed,
Can laugh among the dying, unconcerned.

IV.

Happy the soldier home, with not a notion
How somewhere, every dawn, some men attack,
And many sighs are drained.
Happy the lad whose mind was never trained:
His days are worth forgetting more than not.
He sings along the march
Which we march taciturn, because of dusk,
The long, forlorn, relentless trend
From larger day to huger night.

V.

We wise, who with a thought besmirch
Blood over all our soul,
How should we see our task
But through his blunt and lashless eyes?
Alive, he is not vital overmuch;
Dying, not mortal overmuch;
Nor sad, nor proud,
Nor curious at all.
He cannot tell
Old men's placidity from his.

VI.

But cursed are dullards whom no cannon stuns,
That they should be as stones.
Wretched are they, and mean
With paucity that never was simplicity.
By choice they made themselves immune
To pity and whatever mourns in man

Before the last sea and the hapless stars;
Whatever mourns when many leave these shores;
Whatever shares
The eternal reciprocity of tears.

DULCE ET DECORUM EST

Bent double, like old beggars under sacks,
Knock-kneed, coughing like hags, we cursed through
　　sludge,
Till on the haunting flares we turned our backs,
And towards our distant rest began to trudge.
Men marched asleep. Many had lost their boots,
But limped on, blood-shod. All went lame, all blind;
Drunk with fatigue; deaf even to the hoots
Of gas-shells dropping softly behind.

Gas! GAS! Quick, boys!—An ecstasy of fumbling
Fitting the clumsy helmets just in time,
But someone still was yelling out and stumbling
And flound'ring like a man in fire or lime.—
Dim through the misty panes and thick green light,
As under a green sea, I saw him drowning.

In all my dreams before my helpless sight
He plunges at me, guttering, choking, drowning.

If in some smothering dreams, you too could pace
Behind the wagon that we flung him in,
And watch the white eyes writhing in his face,
His hanging face, like a devil's sick of sin,
If you could hear, at every jolt, the blood
Come gargling from the froth-corrupted lungs
Bitter as the cud
Of vile, incurable sores on innocent tongues,—
My friend, you would not tell with such high zest
To children ardent for some desperate glory,
The old Lie: *Dulce et decorum est
Pro patria mori.*

We'd found an old Boche dug-out, and he knew,
And gave us hell, for shell on frantic shell
Hammered on top, but never quite burst through.
Rain, guttering down in waterfalls of slime
Kept slush waist high, that rising hour by hour,
Choked up the steps too thick with clay to climb.
What murk of air remained stank old, and sour
With fumes of whizz-bangs, and the smell of men
Who'd lived there years, and left their curse in the den,
If not their corpses. . . .
       There we herded from the blast
Of whizz-bangs, but one found our door at last.
Buffeting eyes and breath, snuffing the candles.
And thud! flump! thud! down the steep steps came
    thumping
And splashing in the flood, deluging muck—
The sentry's body; then his rifle, handles
Of old Boche bombs, and mud in ruck on ruck.
We dredged him up, for killed, until he whined
"O sir, my eyes—I'm blind—I'm blind, I'm blind!"
Coaxing, I held a flame against his lids
And said if he could see the least blurred light
He was not blind; in time he'd get all right.
"I can't," he sobbed. Eyeballs, huge-bulged like squids
Watch my dreams still; but I forgot him there
In posting next for duty, and sending a scout
To beg a stretcher somewhere, and floundering about
To other posts under the shrieking air.

Those other wretches, how they bled and spewed,
And one who would have drowned himself for good,—
I try not to remember these things now.
Let dread hark back for one word only: how
Half-listening to that sentry's moans and jumps,
And the wild chattering of his broken teeth,
Renewed most horribly whenever crumps
Pummelled the roof and slogged the air beneath—

Through the dense din, I say, we heard him shout
"I see your lights!" But ours had long died out.

THE DEAD-BEAT

He dropped,—more sullenly than wearily,
Lay stupid like a cod, heavy like meat,
And none of us could kick him to his feet;
Just blinked at my revolver, blearily;
—Didn't appear to know a war was on,
Or see the blasted trench at which he stared.
"I'll do 'em in," he whined, "If this hand's spared,
I'll murder them, I will."

          A low voice said,
"It's Blighty, p'raps, he sees; his pluck's all gone,
Dreaming of all the valiant, that AREN'T dead:
Bold uncles, smiling ministerially;
Maybe his brave young wife, getting her fun
In some new home, improved materially.
It's not these stiffs have crazed him; nor the Hun."

We sent him down at last, out of the way.
Unwounded;—stout lad, too, before that strafe.
Malingering? Stretcher-bearers winked, "Not half!"

Next day I heard the Doc.'s well-whiskied laugh:
"That scum you sent last night soon died. Hooray!"

EXPOSURE

I.

Our brains ache, in the merciless iced east winds that
    knife us . . .
Wearied we keep awake because the night is silent . . .
Low drooping flares confuse our memory of the salient . .
  .

Worried by silence, sentries whisper, curious, nervous,
>   But nothing happens.

Watching, we hear the mad gusts tugging on the wire.
Like twitching agonies of men among its brambles.
Northward incessantly, the flickering gunnery rumbles,
Far off, like a dull rumour of some other war.
>   What are we doing here?

The poignant misery of dawn begins to grow . . .
We only know war lasts, rain soaks, and clouds sag
>   stormy.
Dawn massing in the east her melancholy army
Attacks once more in ranks on shivering ranks of gray,
>   But nothing happens.

Sudden successive flights of bullets streak the silence.
Less deadly than the air that shudders black with snow,
With sidelong flowing flakes that flock, pause and
>   renew,
We watch them wandering up and down the wind's
>   nonchalance,
>   But nothing happens.

II.

Pale flakes with lingering stealth come feeling for our
>   faces—
We cringe in holes, back on forgotten dreams, and stare,
>   snow-dazed,
Deep into grassier ditches. So we drowse, sun-dozed,
Littered with blossoms trickling where the blackbird
>   fusses.
>   Is it that we are dying?

Slowly our ghosts drag home: glimpsing the sunk fires
>   glozed
With crusted dark-red jewels; crickets jingle there;
For hours the innocent mice rejoice: the house is theirs;

Shutters and doors all closed: on us the doors are
    closed—
                We turn back to our dying.

Since we believe not otherwise can kind fires burn;
Nor ever suns smile true on child, or field, or fruit.
For God's invincible spring our love is made afraid;
Therefore, not loath, we lie out here; therefore were born,
        For love of God seems dying.

To-night, His frost will fasten on this mud and us,
Shrivelling many hands and puckering foreheads crisp.
The burying-party, picks and shovels in their shaking
    grasp,
Pause over half-known faces. All their eyes are ice,
        But nothing happens.

SPRING OFFENSIVE

    Halted against the shade of a last hill,
    They fed, and, lying easy, were at ease
    And, finding comfortable chests and knees
    Carelessly slept. But many there stood still
    To face the stark, blank sky beyond the ridge,
    Knowing their feet had come to the end of the world.

    Marvelling they stood, and watched the long grass swirled
    By the May breeze, murmurous with wasp and midge,
    For though the summer oozed into their veins
    Like the injected drug for their bones' pains,
    Sharp on their souls hung the imminent line of grass,
    Fearfully flashed the sky's mysterious glass.

    Hour after hour they ponder the warm field—
    And the far valley behind, where the buttercups
    Had blessed with gold their slow boots coming up,
    Where even the little brambles would not yield,
    But clutched and clung to them like sorrowing hands;
    They breathe like trees unstirred.

Till like a cold gust thrilled the little word
At which each body and its soul begird
And tighten them for battle. No alarms
Of bugles, no high flags, no clamorous haste—
Only a lift and flare of eyes that faced
The sun, like a friend with whom their love is done.
O larger shone that smile against the sun,—
Mightier than his whose bounty these have spurned.

So, soon they topped the hill, and raced together
Over an open stretch of herb and heather
Exposed. And instantly the whole sky burned
With fury against them; and soft sudden cups
Opened in thousands for their blood; and the green
    slopes
Chasmed and steepened sheer to infinite space.

Of them who running on that last high place
Leapt to swift unseen bullets, or went up
On the hot blast and fury of hell's upsurge,
Or plunged and fell away past this world's verge,
Some say God caught them even before they fell.

But what say such as from existence' brink
Ventured but drave too swift to sink.
The few who rushed in the body to enter hell,
And there out-fiending all its fiends and flames
With superhuman inhumanities,
Long-famous glories, immemorial shames
And crawling slowly back, have by degrees
Regained cool peaceful air in wonder—
Why speak they not of comrades that went under?

THE CHANCES

I mind as 'ow the night afore that show
Us five got talking,—we was in the know,
"Over the top to-morrer; boys, we're for it,
First wave we are, first ruddy wave; that's tore it."

53

"Ah well," says Jimmy,—an' 'e's seen some scrappin'—
"There ain't more nor five things as can 'appen;
Ye get knocked out; else wounded—bad or cushy;
Scuppered; or nowt except yer feeling mushy."

One of us got the knock-out, blown to chops.
T'other was hurt, like, losin' both 'is props.
An' one, to use the word of 'ypocrites,
'Ad the misfortoon to be took by Fritz.
Now me, I wasn't scratched, praise God Almighty
(Though next time please I'll thank 'im for a blighty),
But poor young Jim, 'e's livin' an' 'e's not;
'E reckoned 'e'd five chances, an' 'e's 'ad;
'E's wounded, killed, and pris'ner, all the lot—
The ruddy lot all rolled in one. Jim's mad.

S. I. W

"I will to the King,
And offer him consolation in his trouble,
For that man there has set his teeth to die,
And being one that hates obedience,
Discipline, and orderliness of life,
I cannot mourn him."

— W. B. YEATS.

Patting goodbye, doubtless they told the lad
He'd always show the Hun a brave man's face;
Father would sooner him dead than in disgrace,—
Was proud to see him going, aye, and glad.
Perhaps his Mother whimpered how she'd fret
Until he got a nice, safe wound to nurse.
Sisters would wish girls too could shoot, charge, curse, . . .
Brothers—would send his favourite cigarette,
Each week, month after month, they wrote the same,
Thinking him sheltered in some Y.M. Hut,
Where once an hour a bullet missed its aim
And misses teased the hunger of his brain.

His eyes grew old with wincing, and his hand
Reckless with ague. Courage leaked, as sand
From the best sandbags after years of rain.
But never leave, wound, fever, trench-foot, shock,
Untrapped the wretch. And death seemed still withheld
For torture of lying machinally shelled,
At the pleasure of this world's Powers who'd run amok.

He'd seen men shoot their hands, on night patrol,
Their people never knew. Yet they were vile.
"Death sooner than dishonour, that's the style!"
So Father said.

           One dawn, our wire patrol
Carried him. This time, Death had not missed.
We could do nothing, but wipe his bleeding cough.
Could it be accident?—Rifles go off. . .
Not sniped? No. (Later they found the English ball.)

It was the reasoned crisis of his soul.
Against the fires that would not burn him whole
But kept him for death's perjury and scoff
And life's half-promising, and both their riling.

With him they buried the muzzle his teeth had kissed,
And truthfully wrote the Mother "Tim died smiling."

FUTILITY

Move him into the sun—
Gently its touch awoke him once,
At home, whispering of fields unsown.
Always it woke him, even in France,
Until this morning and this snow.
If anything might rouse him now
The kind old sun will know.

Think how it wakes the seeds—
Woke, once, the clays of a cold star.

55

Are limbs so dear-achieved, are sides
Full-nerved,—still warm,—too hard to stir?
Was it for this the clay grew tall?
—O what made fatuous sunbeams toil
To break earth's sleep at all?

SMILE, SMILE, SMILE

Head to limp head, the sunk-eyed wounded scanned
Yesterday's Mail; the casualties (typed small)
And (large) Vast Booty from our Latest Haul.
Also, they read of Cheap Homes, not yet planned;
For, said the paper, "When this war is done
The men's first instinct will be making homes.
Meanwhile their foremost need is aerodromes,
It being certain war has just begun.
Peace would do wrong to our undying dead,—
The sons we offered might regret they died
If we got nothing lasting in their stead.
We must be solidly indemnified.
Though all be worthy Victory which all bought,
We rulers sitting in this ancient spot
Would wrong our very selves if we forgot
The greatest glory will be theirs who fought,
Who kept this nation in integrity."
Nation?—The half-limbed readers did not chafe
But smiled at one another curiously
Like secret men who know their secret safe.
This is the thing they know and never speak,
That England one by one had fled to France
(Not many elsewhere now save under France).
Pictures of these broad smiles appear each week,
And people in whose voice real feeling rings
Say: How they smile! They're happy now, poor things.

23rd September 1918.

CONSCIOUS

His fingers wake, and flutter up the bed.
His eyes come open with a pull of will,
Helped by the yellow may-flowers by his head.
A blind-cord drawls across the window-sill . . .
How smooth the floor of the ward is! what a rug!
And who's that talking, somewhere out of sight?
Why are they laughing? What's inside that jug?
"Nurse! Doctor!" "Yes; all right, all right."

But sudden dusk bewilders all the air—
There seems no time to want a drink of water.
Nurse looks so far away. And everywhere
Music and roses burnt through crimson slaughter.
Cold; cold; he's cold; and yet so hot:
And there's no light to see the voices by—
No time to dream, and ask—he knows not what.

A TERRE

(Being the philosophy of many Soldiers.)

Sit on the bed; I'm blind, and three parts shell,
Be careful; can't shake hands now; never shall.
Both arms have mutinied against me—brutes.
My fingers fidget like ten idle brats.

I tried to peg out soldierly—no use!
One dies of war like any old disease.
This bandage feels like pennies on my eyes.
I have my medals?—Discs to make eyes close.
My glorious ribbons?—Ripped from my own back
In scarlet shreds. (That's for your poetry book.)

A short life and a merry one, my brick!
We used to say we'd hate to live dead old,—
Yet now . . . I'd willingly be puffy, bald,

And patriotic. Buffers catch from boys
At least the jokes hurled at them. I suppose
Little I'd ever teach a son, but hitting,
Shooting, war, hunting, all the arts of hurting.
Well, that's what I learnt,—that, and making money.
Your fifty years ahead seem none too many?
Tell me how long I've got? God! For one year
To help myself to nothing more than air!
One Spring! Is one too good to spare, too long?
Spring wind would work its own way to my lung,
And grow me legs as quick as lilac-shoots.
My servant's lamed, but listen how he shouts!
When I'm lugged out, he'll still be good for that.
Here in this mummy-case, you know, I've thought
How well I might have swept his floors for ever,
I'd ask no night off when the bustle's over,
Enjoying so the dirt. Who's prejudiced
Against a grimed hand when his own's quite dust,
Less live than specks that in the sun-shafts turn,
Less warm than dust that mixes with arms' tan?
I'd love to be a sweep, now, black as Town,
Yes, or a muckman. Must I be his load?

O Life, Life, let me breathe,—a dug-out rat!
Not worse than ours the existences rats lead—
Nosing along at night down some safe vat,
They find a shell-proof home before they rot.
Dead men may envy living mites in cheese,
Or good germs even. Microbes have their joys,
And subdivide, and never come to death,
Certainly flowers have the easiest time on earth.
"I shall be one with nature, herb, and stone."
Shelley would tell me. Shelley would be stunned;
The dullest Tommy hugs that fancy now.
"Pushing up daisies," is their creed, you know.
To grain, then, go my fat, to buds my sap,
For all the usefulness there is in soap.
D'you think the Boche will ever stew man-soup?
Some day, no doubt, if . . .

                    Friend, be very sure
I shall be better off with plants that share
More peaceably the meadow and the shower.
Soft rains will touch me,—as they could touch once,
And nothing but the sun shall make me ware.
Your guns may crash around me. I'll not hear;
Or, if I wince, I shall not know I wince.
Don't take my soul's poor comfort for your jest.
Soldiers may grow a soul when turned to fronds,
But here the thing's best left at home with friends.

My soul's a little grief, grappling your chest,
To climb your throat on sobs; easily chased
On other sighs and wiped by fresher winds.

Carry my crying spirit till it's weaned
To do without what blood remained these wounds.

WILD WITH ALL REGRETS: (ANOTHER VERSION OF "A TERRE".)

To Siegfried Sassoon

My arms have mutinied against me—brutes!
My fingers fidget like ten idle brats,
My back's been stiff for hours, damned hours.
Death never gives his squad a Stand-at-ease.
I can't read. There: it's no use. Take your book.
A short life and a merry one, my buck!
We said we'd hate to grow dead old. But now,
Not to live old seems awful: not to renew
My boyhood with my boys, and teach 'em hitting,
Shooting and hunting,—all the arts of hurting!
—Well, that's what I learnt. That, and making money.
Your fifty years in store seem none too many;
But I've five minutes. God! For just two years
To help myself to this good air of yours!
One Spring! Is one too hard to spare? Too long?
Spring air would find its own way to my lung,

And grow me legs as quick as lilac-shoots.

Yes, there's the orderly. He'll change the sheets
When I'm lugged out, oh, couldn't I do that?
Here in this coffin of a bed, I've thought
I'd like to kneel and sweep his floors for ever,—
And ask no nights off when the bustle's over,
For I'd enjoy the dirt; who's prejudiced
Against a grimed hand when his own's quite dust,—
Less live than specks that in the sun-shafts turn?
Dear dust,—in rooms, on roads, on faces' tan!
I'd love to be a sweep's boy, black as Town;
Yes, or a muckman. Must I be his load?
A flea would do. If one chap wasn't bloody,
Or went stone-cold, I'd find another body.

Which I shan't manage now. Unless it's yours.
I shall stay in you, friend, for some few hours.
You'll feel my heavy spirit chill your chest,
And climb your throat on sobs, until it's chased
On sighs, and wiped from off your lips by wind.

I think on your rich breathing, brother, I'll be weaned
To do without what blood remained me from my wound.

5th December 1917.

DISABLED

He sat in a wheeled chair, waiting for dark,
And shivered in his ghastly suit of grey,
Legless, sewn short at elbow. Through the park
Voices of boys rang saddening like a hymn,
Voices of play and pleasure after day,
Till gathering sleep had mothered them from him.

About this time Town used to swing so gay
When glow-lamps budded in the light-blue trees
And girls glanced lovelier as the air grew dim,

—In the old times, before he threw away his knees.
Now he will never feel again how slim
Girls' waists are, or how warm their subtle hands,
All of them touch him like some queer disease.

There was an artist silly for his face,
For it was younger than his youth, last year.
Now he is old; his back will never brace;
He's lost his colour very far from here,
Poured it down shell-holes till the veins ran dry,
And half his lifetime lapsed in the hot race,
And leap of purple spurted from his thigh.
One time he liked a bloodsmear down his leg,
After the matches carried shoulder-high.
It was after football, when he'd drunk a peg,
He thought he'd better join. He wonders why . . .
Someone had said he'd look a god in kilts.

That's why; and maybe, too, to please his Meg,
Aye, that was it, to please the giddy jilts,
He asked to join. He didn't have to beg;
Smiling they wrote his lie; aged nineteen years.
Germans he scarcely thought of; and no fears
Of Fear came yet. He thought of jewelled hilts
For daggers in plaid socks; of smart salutes;
And care of arms; and leave; and pay arrears;
Esprit de corps; and hints for young recruits.
And soon, he was drafted out with drums and cheers.

Some cheered him home, but not as crowds cheer Goal.
Only a solemn man who brought him fruits
Thanked him; and then inquired about his soul.
Now, he will spend a few sick years in Institutes,
And do what things the rules consider wise,
And take whatever pity they may dole.
To-night he noticed how the women's eyes
Passed from him to the strong men that were whole.
How cold and late it is! Why don't they come
And put him into bed? Why don't they come?

IN FLANDERS FIELDS & OTHER POEMS BY JOHN MCCRAE

IN FLANDERS FIELDS & OTHER POEMS

IN FLANDERS FIELDS

In Flanders fields the poppies blow
Between the crosses, row on row,
That mark our place; and in the sky
The larks, still bravely singing, fly
Scarce heard amid the guns below.

We are the Dead. Short days ago
We lived, felt dawn, saw sunset glow,
Loved and were loved, and now we lie,
        In Flanders fields.

Take up our quarrel with the foe:
To you from failing hands we throw
The torch; be yours to hold it high.
If ye break faith with us who die
We shall not sleep, though poppies grow
        In Flanders fields.

THE ANXIOUS DEAD

O guns, fall silent till the dead men hear

Above their heads the legions pressing on:
(These fought their fight in time of bitter fear,
   And died not knowing how the day had gone.)

O flashing muzzles, pause, and let them see
   The coming dawn that streaks the sky afar;
Then let your mighty chorus witness be
   To them, and Caesar, that we still make war.

Tell them, O guns, that we have heard their call,
   That we have sworn, and will not turn aside,
That we will onward till we win or fall,
   That we will keep the faith for which they died.

Bid them be patient, and some day, anon,
   They shall feel earth enwrapt in silence deep;
Shall greet, in wonderment, the quiet dawn,
   And in content may turn them to their sleep.

THE WARRIOR

He wrought in poverty, the dull grey days,
   But with the night his little lamp-lit room
Was bright with battle flame, or through a haze
   Of smoke that stung his eyes he heard the boom
Of Bluecher's guns; he shared Almeida's scars,
   And from the close-packed deck, about to die,
Looked up and saw the "Birkenhead"'s tall spars
   Weave wavering lines across the Southern sky:

Or in the stifling 'tween decks, row on row,
   At Aboukir, saw how the dead men lay;
Charged with the fiercest in Busaco's strife,
Brave dreams are his — the flick'ring lamp burns low —
Yet couraged for the battles of the day
   He goes to stand full face to face with life.

ISANDLWANA

Scarlet coats, and crash o' the band,
 The grey of a pauper's gown,
A soldier's grave in Zululand,
 And a woman in Brecon Town.

My little lad for a soldier boy,
 (Mothers o' Brecon Town!)
My eyes for tears and his for joy
 When he went from Brecon Town,
His for the flags and the gallant sights
His for the medals and his for the fights,
And mine for the dreary, rainy nights
 At home in Brecon Town.

They say he's laid beneath a tree,
 (Come back to Brecon Town!)
Shouldn't I know? — I was there to see:
 (It's far to Brecon Town!)
It's me that keeps it trim and drest
With a briar there and a rose by his breast —
The English flowers he likes the best
 That I bring from Brecon Town.

And I sit beside him — him and me,
 (We're back to Brecon Town.)
To talk of the things that used to be
 (Grey ghosts of Brecon Town);
I know the look o' the land and sky,
And the bird that builds in the tree near by,
And times I hear the jackals cry,
 And me in Brecon Town.

Golden grey on miles of sand
 The dawn comes creeping down;
It's day in far off Zululand
 And night in Brecon Town.

THE UNCONQUERED DEAD

". . . defeated, with great loss."

Not we the conquered! Not to us the blame
   Of them that flee, of them that basely yield;
Nor ours the shout of victory, the fame
   Of them that vanquish in a stricken field.

That day of battle in the dusty heat
   We lay and heard the bullets swish and sing
Like scythes amid the over-ripened wheat,
   And we the harvest of their garnering.

Some yielded, No, not we! Not we, we swear
   By these our wounds; this trench upon the hill
Where all the shell-strewn earth is seamed and bare,
   Was ours to keep; and lo! we have it still.

We might have yielded, even we, but death
   Came for our helper; like a sudden flood
The crashing darkness fell; our painful breath
   We drew with gasps amid the choking blood.

The roar fell faint and farther off, and soon
   Sank to a foolish humming in our ears,
Like crickets in the long, hot afternoon
   Among the wheat fields of the olden years.

Before our eyes a boundless wall of red
   Shot through by sudden streaks of jagged pain!
Then a slow-gathering darkness overhead
   And rest came on us like a quiet rain.

Not we the conquered! Not to us the shame,
   Who hold our earthen ramparts, nor shall cease
To hold them ever; victors we, who came
   In that fierce moment to our honoured peace.

THE CAPTAIN: 1797

Here all the day she swings from tide to tide,
Here all night long she tugs a rusted chain,
A masterless hulk that was a ship of pride,
Yet unashamed: her memories remain.

It was Nelson in the *Captain*, Cape St. Vincent far alee,
  With the *Vanguard* leading s'uth'ard in the haze —
Little Jervis and the Spaniards and the fight that was
      to be,
Twenty-seven Spanish battleships, great bullies of the sea,
  And the *Captain* there to find her day of days.

Right into them the *Vanguard* leads, but with a
      sudden tack
  The Spaniards double swiftly on their trail;
Now Jervis overshoots his mark, like some too eager pack,
He will not overtake them, haste he e'er so greatly back,
  But Nelson and the *Captain* will not fail.

Like a tigress on her quarry leaps the *Captain* from her
      place,
  To lie across the fleeing squadron's way:
Heavy odds and heavy onslaught, gun to gun and face to
      face,
Win the ship a name of glory, win the men a death of
      grace,
  For a little hold the Spanish fleet in play.

Ended now the *Captain's* battle, stricken sore she falls aside
  Holding still her foemen, beaten to the knee:
As the *Vanguard* drifted past her, "Well done, *Captain*,"
      Jervis cried,
Rang the cheers of men that conquered, ran the blood of
      men that died,
  And the ship had won her immortality.

Lo! here her progeny of steel and steam,

A funnelled monster at her mooring swings:
Still, in our hearts, we see her pennant stream,
And "Well done, Captain," like a trumpet rings.

THE SONG OF THE DERELICT

Ye have sung me your songs, ye have chanted your rimes
  (I scorn your beguiling, O sea!)
Ye fondle me now, but to strike me betimes.
  (A treacherous lover, the sea!)
Once I saw as I lay, half-awash in the night
A hull in the gloom — a quick hail — and a light
And I lurched o'er to leeward and saved her for spite
  From the doom that ye meted to me.

I was sister to 'Terrible', seventy-four,
  (Yo ho! for the swing of the sea!)
And ye sank her in fathoms a thousand or more
  (Alas! for the might of the sea!)
Ye taunt me and sing me her fate for a sign!
What harm can ye wreak more on me or on mine?
Ho braggart! I care not for boasting of thine —
  A fig for the wrath of the sea!

Some night to the lee of the land I shall steal,
  (Heigh-ho to be home from the sea!)
No pilot but Death at the rudderless wheel,
  (None knoweth the harbor as he!)
To lie where the slow tide creeps hither and fro
And the shifting sand laps me around, for I know
That my gallant old crew are in Port long ago —
  For ever at peace with the sea!

QUEBEC: 1608-1908

Of old, like Helen, guerdon of the strong —
  Like Helen fair, like Helen light of word, —
"The spoils unto the conquerors belong.

Who winneth me must win me by the sword."

Grown old, like Helen, once the jealous prize
  That strong men battled for in savage hate,
Can she look forth with unregretful eyes,
  Where sleep Montcalm and Wolfe beside her gate?

THEN AND NOW

Beneath her window in the fragrant night
  I half forget how truant years have flown
Since I looked up to see her chamber-light,
  Or catch, perchance, her slender shadow thrown
Upon the casement; but the nodding leaves
  Sweep lazily across the unlit pane,
And to and fro beneath the shadowy eaves,
  Like restless birds, the breath of coming rain
Creeps, lilac-laden, up the village street
  When all is still, as if the very trees
Were listening for the coming of her feet
  That come no more; yet, lest I weep, the breeze
Sings some forgotten song of those old years
Until my heart grows far too glad for tears.

UNSOLVED

Amid my books I lived the hurrying years,
  Disdaining kinship with my fellow man,
Alike to me were human smiles and tears,
  I cared not whither Earth's great life-stream ran,
Till as I knelt before my mouldered shrine,
  God made me look into a woman's eyes;
And I, who thought all earthly wisdom mine,
  Knew in a moment that the eternal skies
Were measured but in inches, to the quest
  That lay before me in that mystic gaze.
"Surely I have been errant: it is best
  That I should tread, with men their human ways."

God took the teacher, ere the task was learned,
And to my lonely books again I turned.

THE HOPE OF MY HEART

"Delicta juventutis et ignorantius ejus,
quoesumus ne memineris, Domine."

I left, to earth, a little maiden fair,
    With locks of gold, and eyes that shamed the light;
I prayed that God might have her in His care
  And sight.

Earth's love was false; her voice, a siren's song;
    (Sweet mother-earth was but a lying name)
The path she showed was but the path of wrong
  And shame.

"Cast her not out!" I cry. God's kind words come —
    "Her future is with Me, as was her past;
It shall be My good will to bring her home
        At last."

PENANCE

My lover died a century ago,
Her dear heart stricken by my sland'rous breath,
Wherefore the Gods forbade that I should know
        The peace of death.

Men pass my grave, and say, "'Twere well to sleep,
Like such an one, amid the uncaring dead!"
How should they know the vigils that I keep,
        The tears I shed?

Upon the grave, I count with lifeless breath,

Each night, each year, the flowers that bloom and die,
Deeming the leaves, that fall to dreamless death,
                    More blest than I.

'Twas just last year — I heard two lovers pass
So near, I caught the tender words he said:
To-night the rain-drenched breezes sway the grass
                    Above his head.

That night full envious of his life was I,
That youth and love should stand at his behest;
To-night, I envy him, that he should lie
                    At utter rest.

SLUMBER SONGS

I

Sleep, little eyes
That brim with childish tears amid thy play,
Be comforted! No grief of night can weigh
Against the joys that throng thy coming day.

Sleep, little heart!
There is no place in Slumberland for tears:
Life soon enough will bring its chilling fears
And sorrows that will dim the after years.
Sleep, little heart!

II

Ah, little eyes
Dead blossoms of a springtime long ago,
That life's storm crushed and left to lie below
The benediction of the falling snow!

Sleep, little heart
That ceased so long ago its frantic beat!
The years that come and go with silent feet

73

Have naught to tell save this — that rest is sweet.
Dear little heart.

THE OLDEST DRAMA

*"It fell on a day, that he went out to his father to the reapers. And he said
unto his father, My head, my head. And he said to a lad, Carry him to his
mother. And . . . he sat on her knees till noon, and then died. And she
went up, and laid him on the bed. . . . And shut the door upon him and
went out."*

Immortal story that no mother's heart
    Ev'n yet can read, nor feel the biting pain
That rent her soul! Immortal not by art
    Which makes a long past sorrow sting again

Like grief of yesterday: but since it said
    In simplest word the truth which all may see,
Where any mother sobs above her dead
    And plays anew the silent tragedy.

RECOMPENSE

I saw two sowers in Life's field at morn,
    To whom came one in angel guise and said,
"Is it for labour that a man is born?
    Lo: I am Ease. Come ye and eat my bread!"
Then gladly one forsook his task undone
    And with the Tempter went his slothful way,
The other toiled until the setting sun
    With stealing shadows blurred the dusty day.

Ere harvest time, upon earth's peaceful breast
    Each laid him down among the unreaping dead.
"Labour hath other recompense than rest,
    Else were the toiler like the fool," I said;
"God meteth him not less, but rather more
Because he sowed and others reaped his store."

MINE HOST

There stands a hostel by a travelled way;
    Life is the road and Death the worthy host;
Each guest he greets, nor ever lacks to say,
    "How have ye fared?" They answer him, the most,
"This lodging place is other than we sought;
    We had intended farther, but the gloom
Came on apace, and found us ere we thought:
    Yet will we lodge. Thou hast abundant room."

Within sit haggard men that speak no word,
    No fire gleams their cheerful welcome shed;
No voice of fellowship or strife is heard
    But silence of a multitude of dead.
"Naught can I offer ye," quoth Death, "but rest!"
And to his chamber leads each tired guest.

EQUALITY

I saw a King, who spent his life to weave
    Into a nation all his great heart thought,
Unsatisfied until he should achieve
    The grand ideal that his manhood sought;
Yet as he saw the end within his reach,
    Death took the sceptre from his failing hand,
And all men said, "He gave his life to teach
    The task of honour to a sordid land!"
Within his gates I saw, through all those years,
    One at his humble toil with cheery face,
Whom (being dead) the children, half in tears,
    Remembered oft, and missed him from his place.
If he be greater that his people blessed
Than he the children loved, God knoweth best.

ANARCHY

I saw a city filled with lust and shame,

Where men, like wolves, slunk through the grim half-
    light;
And sudden, in the midst of it, there came
    One who spoke boldly for the cause of Right.

And speaking, fell before that brutish race
    Like some poor wren that shrieking eagles tear,
While brute Dishonour, with her bloodless face
    Stood by and smote his lips that moved in prayer.

"Speak not of God! In centuries that word
    Hath not been uttered! Our own king are we."
And God stretched forth his finger as He heard
    And o'er it cast a thousand leagues of sea.

DISARMAMENT

One spake amid the nations, "Let us cease
    From darkening with strife the fair World's light,
We who are great in war be great in peace.
    No longer let us plead the cause by might."

But from a million British graves took birth
    A silent voice — the million spake as one —
"If ye have righted all the wrongs of earth
    Lay by the sword! Its work and ours is done."

THE DEAD MASTER

Amid earth's vagrant noises, he caught the note sublime:
To-day around him surges from the silences of Time
A flood of nobler music, like a river deep and broad,
Fit song for heroes gathered in the banquet-hall of God.

THE HARVEST OF THE SEA

The earth grows white with harvest; all day long
    The sickles gleam, until the darkness weaves

Her web of silence o'er the thankful song
    Of reapers bringing home the golden sheaves.

The wave tops whiten on the sea fields drear,
    And men go forth at haggard dawn to reap;
But ever 'mid the gleaners' song we hear
    The half-hushed sobbing of the hearts that weep.

THE DYING OF PERE PIERRE

*". . . with two other priests; the same night he died, and was buried
   by the shores of the lake that bears his name."*

— CHRONICLE

"Nay, grieve not that ye can no honour give
    To these poor bones that presently must be
But carrion; since I have sought to live
    Upon God's earth, as He hath guided me,
I shall not lack! Where would ye have me lie?
    High heaven is higher than cathedral nave:
Do men paint chancels fairer than the sky?"
    Beside the darkened lake they made his grave,
Below the altar of the hills; and night
    Swung incense clouds of mist in creeping lines
That twisted through the tree-trunks, where the light
    Groped through the arches of the silent pines:
And he, beside the lonely path he trod,
Lay, tombed in splendour, in the House of God.

EVENTIDE

The day is past and the toilers cease;
The land grows dim 'mid the shadows grey,
And hearts are glad, for the dark brings peace
    At the close of day.

Each weary toiler, with lingering pace,

As he homeward turns, with the long day done,
Looks out to the west, with the light on his face
       Of the setting sun.

Yet some see not (with their sin-dimmed eyes)
The promise of rest in the fading light;
But the clouds loom dark in the angry skies
       At the fall of night.

And some see only a golden sky
Where the elms their welcoming arms stretch wide
To the calling rooks, as they homeward fly
       At the eventide.

It speaks of peace that comes after strife,
Of the rest He sends to the hearts He tried,
Of the calm that follows the stormiest life —
       God's eventide.

UPON WATTS' PICTURE "SIC TRANSIT"

"What I spent I had; what I saved, I lost; what I gave, I have."

But yesterday the tourney, all the eager joy of life,
   The waving of the banners, and the rattle of the
     spears,
The clash of sword and harness, and the madness of the
     strife;
   To-night begin the silence and the peace of endless
     years.

(One sings within.)

But yesterday the glory and the prize,
   And best of all, to lay it at her feet,
To find my guerdon in her speaking eyes:
   I grudge them not, — they pass, albeit sweet.

The ring of spears, the winning of the fight,

The careless song, the cup, the love of friends,
The earth in spring — to live, to feel the light —
 'Twas good the while it lasted: here it ends.

Remain the well-wrought deed in honour done,
 The dole for Christ's dear sake, the words that fall
In kindliness upon some outcast one, —
 They seemed so little: now they are my All.

A SONG OF COMFORT

"Sleep, weary ones, while ye may —
 Sleep, oh, sleep!"

— EUGENE FIELD

Thro' May time blossoms, with whisper low,
The soft wind sang to the dead below:
"Think not with regret on the Springtime's song
And the task ye left while your hands were strong.
The song would have ceased when the Spring was past,
And the task that was joyous be weary at last."

To the winter sky when the nights were long
The tree-tops tossed with a ceaseless song:
"Do ye think with regret on the sunny days
And the path ye left, with its untrod ways?
The sun might sink in a storm cloud's frown
And the path grow rough when the night came down."

In the grey twilight of the autumn eves,
It sighed as it sang through the dying leaves:
 "Ye think with regret that the world was bright,
 That your path was short and your task was light;
 The path, though short, was perhaps the best
 And the toil was sweet, that it led to rest."

THE PILGRIMS

An uphill path, sun-gleams between the showers,
　　Where every beam that broke the leaden sky
Lit other hills with fairer ways than ours;
　　Some clustered graves where half our memories lie;
And one grim Shadow creeping ever nigh:
　　　　And this was Life.

Wherein we did another's burden seek,
　　The tired feet we helped upon the road,
The hand we gave the weary and the weak,
　　The miles we lightened one another's load,
When, faint to falling, onward yet we strode:
　　　　This too was Life.

Till, at the upland, as we turned to go
　　Amid fair meadows, dusky in the night,
The mists fell back upon the road below;
　　Broke on our tired eyes the western light;
The very graves were for a moment bright:
　　　　And this was Death.

THE SHADOW OF THE CROSS

At the drowsy dusk when the shadows creep
From the golden west, where the sunbeams sleep,

An angel mused: "Is there good or ill
In the mad world's heart, since on Calvary's hill

'Round the cross a mid-day twilight fell
That darkened earth and o'ershadowed hell?"

Through the streets of a city the angel sped;
Like an open scroll men's hearts he read.

In a monarch's ear his courtiers lied

And humble faces hid hearts of pride.

Men's hate waxed hot, and their hearts grew cold,
As they haggled and fought for the lust of gold.

Despairing, he cried, "After all these years
Is there naught but hatred and strife and tears?"

He found two waifs in an attic bare;
— A single crust was their meagre fare —

One strove to quiet the other's cries,
And the love-light dawned in her famished eyes

As she kissed the child with a motherly air:
"I don't need mine, you can have my share."

Then the angel knew that the earthly cross
And the sorrow and shame were not wholly loss.

At dawn, when hushed was earth's busy hum
And men looked not for their Christ to come,

From the attic poor to the palace grand,
The King and the beggar went hand in hand.

THE NIGHT COMETH

Cometh the night. The wind falls low,
The trees swing slowly to and fro:
Around the church the headstones grey
Cluster, like children strayed away
But found again, and folded so.

No chiding look doth she bestow:
If she is glad, they cannot know;
    If ill or well they spend their day,
            Cometh the night.

Singing or sad, intent they go;
They do not see the shadows grow;
"There yet is time," they lightly say,
"Before our work aside we lay";
   Their task is but half-done, and lo!
       Cometh the night.

IN DUE SEASON

If night should come and find me at my toil,
  When all Life's day I had, tho' faintly, wrought,
And shallow furrows, cleft in stony soil
  Were all my labour: Shall I count it naught

If only one poor gleaner, weak of hand,
  Shall pick a scanty sheaf where I have sown?
"Nay, for of thee the Master doth demand
  Thy work: the harvest rests with Him alone."

WARTIME POEMS OF ALAN SEEGER

LAST POEMS

THE AISNE (1914-15)

We first saw fire on the tragic slopes
  Where the flood-tide of France's early gain,
Big with wrecked promise and abandoned hopes,
  Broke in a surf of blood along the Aisne.

The charge her heroes left us, we assumed,
  What, dying, they reconquered, we preserved,
In the chill trenches, harried, shelled, entombed,
  Winter came down on us, but no man swerved.

Winter came down on us. The low clouds, torn
  In the stark branches of the riven pines,
Blurred the white rockets that from dusk till morn
  Traced the wide curve of the close-grappling lines.

In rain, and fog that on the withered hill
  Froze before dawn, the lurking foe drew down;
Or light snows fell that made forlorner still
  The ravaged country and the ruined town;

Or the long clouds would end. Intensely fair,
  The winter constellations blazing forth —

Perseus, the Twins, Orion, the Great Bear —
  Gleamed on our bayonets pointing to the north.

And the lone sentinel would start and soar
  On wings of strong emotion as he knew
That kinship with the stars that only War
  Is great enough to lift man's spirit to.

And ever down the curving front, aglow
  With the pale rockets' intermittent light,
He heard, like distant thunder, growl and grow
  The rumble of far battles in the night, —

Rumors, reverberant, indistinct, remote,
  Borne from red fields whose martial names have won
The power to thrill like a far trumpet-note, —
  Vic, Vailly, Soupir, Hurtelise, Craonne . . .

Craonne, before thy cannon-swept plateau,
  Where like sere leaves lay strewn September's dead,
  I found for all dear things I forfeited
A recompense I would not now forego.

For that high fellowship was ours then
  With those who, championing another's good,
  More than dull Peace or its poor votaries could,
Taught us the dignity of being men.

There we drained deeper the deep cup of life,
  And on sublimer summits came to learn,
  After soft things, the terrible and stern,
After sweet Love, the majesty of Strife;

There where we faced under those frowning heights
  The blast that maims, the hurricane that kills;
  There where the watchlights on the winter hills
Flickered like balefire through inclement nights;

There where, firm links in the unyielding chain,

Where fell the long-planned blow and fell in vain —
  Hearts worthy of the honor and the trial,
We helped to hold the lines along the Aisne.

CHAMPAGNE (1914-15)

In the glad revels, in the happy fetes,
  When cheeks are flushed, and glasses gilt and pearled
With the sweet wine of France that concentrates
  The sunshine and the beauty of the world,

Drink sometimes, you whose footsteps yet may tread
  The undisturbed, delightful paths of Earth,
To those whose blood, in pious duty shed,
  Hallows the soil where that same wine had birth.

Here, by devoted comrades laid away,
  Along our lines they slumber where they fell,
Beside the crater at the Ferme d'Alger
  And up the bloody slopes of La Pompelle,

And round the city whose cathedral towers
  The enemies of Beauty dared profane,
And in the mat of multicolored flowers
  That clothe the sunny chalk-fields of Champagne.

Under the little crosses where they rise
  The soldier rests. Now round him undismayed
The cannon thunders, and at night he lies
  At peace beneath the eternal fusillade. . . .

That other generations might possess —
  From shame and menace free in years to come —
A richer heritage of happiness,
  He marched to that heroic martyrdom.

Esteeming less the forfeit that he paid
  Than undishonored that his flag might float
Over the towers of liberty, he made

His breast the bulwark and his blood the moat.

Obscurely sacrificed, his nameless tomb,
  Bare of the sculptor's art, the poet's lines,
Summer shall flush with poppy-fields in bloom,
  And Autumn yellow with maturing vines.

There the grape-pickers at their harvesting
  Shall lightly tread and load their wicker trays,
Blessing his memory as they toil and sing
  In the slant sunshine of October days. . . .

I love to think that if my blood should be
  So privileged to sink where his has sunk,
I shall not pass from Earth entirely,
  But when the banquet rings, when healths are drunk,

And faces that the joys of living fill
  Glow radiant with laughter and good cheer,
In beaming cups some spark of me shall still
  Brim toward the lips that once I held so dear.

So shall one coveting no higher plane
  Than nature clothes in color and flesh and tone,
Even from the grave put upward to attain
  The dreams youth cherished and missed and might have
    known;

And that strong need that strove unsatisfied
  Toward earthly beauty in all forms it wore,
Not death itself shall utterly divide
  From the beloved shapes it thirsted for.

Alas, how many an adept for whose arms
  Life held delicious offerings perished here,
How many in the prime of all that charms,
  Crowned with all gifts that conquer and endear!

Honor them not so much with tears and flowers,

But you with whom the sweet fulfilment lies,
Where in the anguish of atrocious hours
  Turned their last thoughts and closed their dying eyes,

Rather when music on bright gatherings lays
  Its tender spell, and joy is uppermost,
Be mindful of the men they were, and raise
  Your glasses to them in one silent toast.

Drink to them—amorous of dear Earth as well,
  They asked no tribute lovelier than this —
And in the wine that ripened where they fell,
  Oh, frame your lips as though it were a kiss.

Champagne, France, July, 1915.

THE HOSTS

Purged, with the life they left, of all
That makes life paltry and mean and small,
In their new dedication charged
With something heightened, enriched, enlarged,
That lends a light to their lusty brows
And a song to the rhythm of their tramping feet,
These are the men that have taken vows,
These are the hardy, the flower, the elite, —
These are the men that are moved no more
By the will to traffic and grasp and store
And ring with pleasure and wealth and love
The circles that self is the center of;
But they are moved by the powers that force
The sea forever to ebb and rise,
That hold Arcturus in his course,
And marshal at noon in tropic skies
The clouds that tower on some snow-capped chain
And drift out over the peopled plain.
They are big with the beauty of cosmic things.
Mark how their columns surge! They seem
To follow the goddess with outspread wings

That points toward Glory, the soldier's dream.
With bayonets bare and flags unfurled,
They scale the summits of the world
And fade on the farthest golden height
In fair horizons full of light.

    Comrades in arms there—friend or foe —
That trod the perilous, toilsome trail
Through a world of ruin and blood and woe
In the years of the great decision—hail!
Friend or foe, it shall matter nought;
This only matters, in fine: we fought.
For we were young and in love or strife
Sought exultation and craved excess:
To sound the wildest debauch in life
We staked our youth and its loveliness.
Let idlers argue the right and wrong
And weigh what merit our causes had.
Putting our faith in being strong —
Above the level of good and bad —
For us, we battled and burned and killed
Because evolving Nature willed,
And it was our pride and boast to be
The instruments of Destiny.
There was a stately drama writ
By the hand that peopled the earth and air
And set the stars in the infinite
And made night gorgeous and morning fair,
And all that had sense to reason knew
That bloody drama must be gone through.
Some sat and watched how the action veered —
Waited, profited, trembled, cheered —
We saw not clearly nor understood,
But yielding ourselves to the masterhand,
Each in his part as best he could,
We played it through as the author planned.

A shell surprised our post one day
  And killed a comrade at my side.
My heart was sick to see the way
    He suffered as he died.

I dug about the place he fell,
  And found, no bigger than my thumb,
A fragment of the splintered shell
    In warm aluminum.

I melted it, and made a mould,
  And poured it in the opening,
And worked it, when the cast was cold,
    Into a shapely ring.

And when my ring was smooth and bright,
  Holding it on a rounded stick,
For seal, I bade a Turco write
    'Maktoob' in Arabic.

'Maktoob!' "'Tis written!" . . . So they think,
  These children of the desert, who
From its immense expanses drink
    Some of its grandeur too.

Within the book of Destiny,
  Whose leaves are time, whose cover, space,
The day when you shall cease to be,
    The hour, the mode, the place,

Are marked, they say; and you shall not
  By taking thought or using wit
Alter that certain fate one jot,
    Postpone or conjure it.

Learn to drive fear, then, from your heart.
  If you must perish, know, O man,

'Tis an inevitable part
    Of the predestined plan.

And, seeing that through the ebon door
    Once only you may pass, and meet
Of those that have gone through before
    The mighty, the elite ——

Guard that not bowed nor blanched with fear
    You enter, but serene, erect,
As you would wish most to appear
    To those you most respect.

So die as though your funeral
    Ushered you through the doors that led
Into a stately banquet hall
    Where heroes banqueted;

And it shall all depend therein
    Whether you come as slave or lord,
If they acclaim you as their kin
    Or spurn you from their board.

So, when the order comes: "Attack!"
    And the assaulting wave deploys,
And the heart trembles to look back
    On life and all its joys;

Or in a ditch that they seem near
    To find, and round your shallow trough
Drop the big shells that you can hear
    Coming a half mile off;

When, not to hear, some try to talk,
    And some to clean their guns, or sing,
And some dig deeper in the chalk ——
    I look upon my ring:

And nerves relax that were most tense,

And Death comes whistling down unheard,
As I consider all the sense
  Held in that mystic word.

And it brings, quieting like balm
  My heart whose flutterings have ceased,
The resignation and the calm
  And wisdom of the East.

I HAVE A RENDEZVOUS WITH DEATH . . .

I have a rendezvous with Death
At some disputed barricade,
When Spring comes back with rustling shade
And apple-blossoms fill the air —
I have a rendezvous with Death
When Spring brings back blue days and fair.

  It may be he shall take my hand
And lead me into his dark land
And close my eyes and quench my breath —
It may be I shall pass him still.
I have a rendezvous with Death
On some scarred slope of battered hill,
When Spring comes round again this year
And the first meadow-flowers appear.

  God knows 'twere better to be deep
Pillowed in silk and scented down,
Where Love throbs out in blissful sleep,
Pulse nigh to pulse, and breath to breath,
Where hushed awakenings are dear . . .
But I've a rendezvous with Death
At midnight in some flaming town,
When Spring trips north again this year,
And I to my pledged word am true,
I shall not fail that rendezvous.

SONNETS

SONNET I

Sidney, in whom the heyday of romance
Came to its precious and most perfect flower,
Whether you tourneyed with victorious lance
Or brought sweet roundelays to Stella's bower,
I give myself some credit for the way
I have kept clean of what enslaves and lowers,
Shunned the ideals of our present day
And studied those that were esteemed in yours;
For, turning from the mob that buys Success
By sacrificing all Life's better part,
Down the free roads of human happiness
I frolicked, poor of purse but light of heart,
And lived in strict devotion all along
To my three idols—Love and Arms and Song.

SONNET II

Not that I always struck the proper mean
Of what mankind must give for what they gain,
But, when I think of those whom dull routine
And the pursuit of cheerless toil enchain,

Who from their desk-chairs seeing a summer cloud
Race through blue heaven on its joyful course
Sigh sometimes for a life less cramped and bowed,
I think I might have done a great deal worse;
For I have ever gone untied and free,
The stars and my high thoughts for company;
Wet with the salt-spray and the mountain showers,
I have had the sense of space and amplitude,
And love in many places, silver-shoed,
Has come and scattered all my path with flowers.

SONNET III

Why should you be astonished that my heart,
Plunged for so long in darkness and in dearth,
Should be revived by you, and stir and start
As by warm April now, reviving Earth?
I am the field of undulating grass
And you the gentle perfumed breath of Spring,
And all my lyric being, when you pass,
Is bowed and filled with sudden murmuring.
I asked you nothing and expected less,
But, with that deep, impassioned tenderness
Of one approaching what he most adores,
I only wished to lose a little space
All thought of my own life, and in its place
To live and dream and have my joy in yours.

SONNET IV: TO . . . IN CHURCH

If I was drawn here from a distant place,
'Twas not to pray nor hear our friend's address,
But, gazing once more on your winsome face,
To worship there Ideal Loveliness.
On that pure shrine that has too long ignored
The gifts that once I brought so frequently
I lay this votive offering, to record
How sweet your quiet beauty seemed to me.

Enchanting girl, my faith is not a thing
By futile prayers and vapid psalm-singing
To vent in crowded nave and public pew.
My creed is simple: that the world is fair,
And beauty the best thing to worship there,
And I confess it by adoring you.

Biarritz, Sunday, March 26, 1916.

SONNET V

Seeing you have not come with me, nor spent
This day's suggestive beauty as we ought,
I have gone forth alone and been content
To make you mistress only of my thought.
And I have blessed the fate that was so kind
In my life's agitations to include
This moment's refuge where my sense can find
Refreshment, and my soul beatitude.
Oh, be my gentle love a little while!
Walk with me sometimes. Let me see you smile.
Watching some night under a wintry sky,
Before the charge, or on the bed of pain,
These blessed memories shall revive again
And be a power to cheer and fortify.

SONNET VI

Oh, you are more desirable to me
Than all I staked in an impulsive hour,
Making my youth the sport of chance, to be
Blighted or torn in its most perfect flower;
For I think less of what that chance may bring
Than how, before returning into fire,
To make my dearest memory of the thing
That is but now my ultimate desire.
And in old times I should have prayed to her
Whose haunt the groves of windy Cyprus were,

To prosper me and crown with good success
My will to make of you the rose-twined bowl
From whose inebriating brim my soul
Shall drink its last of earthly happiness.

SONNET VII

There have been times when I could storm and plead,
But you shall never hear me supplicate.
These long months that have magnified my need
Have made my asking less importunate,
For now small favors seem to me so great
That not the courteous lovers of old time
Were more content to rule themselves and wait,
Easing desire with discourse and sweet rhyme.
Nay, be capricious, willful; have no fear
To wound me with unkindness done or said,
Lest mutual devotion make too dear
My life that hangs by a so slender thread,
And happy love unnerve me before May
For that stern part that I have yet to play.

SONNET VIII

Oh, love of woman, you are known to be
A passion sent to plague the hearts of men;
For every one you bring felicity
Bringing rebuffs and wretchedness to ten.
I have been oft where human life sold cheap
And seen men's brains spilled out about their ears
And yet that never cost me any sleep;
I lived untroubled and I shed no tears.
Fools prate how war is an atrocious thing;
I always knew that nothing it implied
Equalled the agony of suffering
Of him who loves and loves unsatisfied.
War is a refuge to a heart like this;
Love only tells it what true torture is.

SONNET IX

Well, seeing I have no hope, then let us part;
Having long taught my flesh to master fear,
I should have learned by now to rule my heart,
Although, Heaven knows, 'tis not so easy near.
Oh, you were made to make men miserable
And torture those who would have joy in you,
But I, who could have loved you, dear, so well,
Take pride in being a good loser too;
And it has not been wholly unsuccess,
For I have rescued from forgetfulness
Some moments of this precious time that flies,
Adding to my past wealth of memory
The pretty way you once looked up at me,
Your low, sweet voice, your smile, and your dear eyes.

SONNET X

I have sought Happiness, but it has been
A lovely rainbow, baffling all pursuit,
And tasted Pleasure, but it was a fruit
More fair of outward hue than sweet within.
Renouncing both, a flake in the ferment
Of battling hosts that conquer or recoil,
There only, chastened by fatigue and toil,
I knew what came the nearest to content.
For there at least my troubled flesh was free
From the gadfly Desire that plagued it so;
Discord and Strife were what I used to know,
Heartaches, deception, murderous jealousy;
By War transported far from all of these,
Amid the clash of arms I was at peace.

SONNET XI: ON RETURNING TO THE FRONT AFTER LEAVE

Apart sweet women (for whom Heaven be blessed),

Comrades, you cannot think how thin and blue
Look the leftovers of mankind that rest,
Now that the cream has been skimmed off in you.
War has its horrors, but has this of good —
That its sure processes sort out and bind
Brave hearts in one intrepid brotherhood
And leave the shams and imbeciles behind.
Now turn we joyful to the great attacks,
Not only that we face in a fair field
Our valiant foe and all his deadly tools,
But also that we turn disdainful backs
On that poor world we scorn yet die to shield —
That world of cowards, hypocrites, and fools.

SONNET XII

Clouds rosy-tinted in the setting sun,
Depths of the azure eastern sky between,
Plains where the poplar-bordered highways run,
Patched with a hundred tints of brown and green, —
Beauty of Earth, when in thy harmonies
The cannon's note has ceased to be a part,
I shall return once more and bring to these
The worship of an undivided heart.
Of those sweet potentialities that wait
For my heart's deep desire to fecundate
I shall resume the search, if Fortune grants;
And the great cities of the world shall yet
Be golden frames for me in which to set
New masterpieces of more rare romance.

OTHER POEMS

BELLINGLISE

I

Deep in the sloping forest that surrounds
The head of a green valley that I know,
Spread the fair gardens and ancestral grounds
Of Bellinglise, the beautiful chateau.
Through shady groves and fields of unmown grass,
It was my joy to come at dusk and see,
Filling a little pond's untroubled glass,
Its antique towers and mouldering masonry.
Oh, should I fall to-morrow, lay me here,
That o'er my tomb, with each reviving year,
Wood-flowers may blossom and the wood-doves croon;
And lovers by that unrecorded place,
Passing, may pause, and cling a little space,
Close-bosomed, at the rising of the moon.

II

Here, where in happier times the huntsman's horn
Echoing from far made sweet midsummer eves,
Now serried cannon thunder night and morn,

Tearing with iron the greenwood's tender leaves.
Yet has sweet Spring no particle withdrawn
Of her old bounty; still the song-birds hail,
Even through our fusillade, delightful Dawn;
Even in our wire bloom lilies of the vale.
You who love flowers, take these; their fragile bells
Have trembled with the shock of volleyed shells,
And in black nights when stealthy foes advance
They have been lit by the pale rockets' glow
That o'er scarred fields and ancient towns laid low
Trace in white fire the brave frontiers of France.

May 22, 1916.

LIEBESTOD

I who, conceived beneath another star,
Had been a prince and played with life, instead
Have been its slave, an outcast exiled far
From the fair things my faith has merited.
My ways have been the ways that wanderers tread
And those that make romance of poverty —
Soldier, I shared the soldier's board and bed,
And Joy has been a thing more oft to me
Whispered by summer wind and summer sea
Than known incarnate in the hours it lies
All warm against our hearts and laughs into our eyes.

I know not if in risking my best days
I shall leave utterly behind me here
This dream that lightened me through lonesome ways
And that no disappointment made less dear;
Sometimes I think that, where the hilltops rear
Their white entrenchments back of tangled wire,
Behind the mist Death only can make clear,
There, like Brunhilde ringed with flaming fire,
Lies what shall ease my heart's immense desire:
There, where beyond the horror and the pain
Only the brave shall pass, only the strong attain.

Truth or delusion, be it as it may,
Yet think it true, dear friends, for, thinking so,
That thought shall nerve our sinews on the day
When to the last assault our bugles blow:
Reckless of pain and peril we shall go,
Heads high and hearts aflame and bayonets bare,
And we shall brave eternity as though
Eyes looked on us in which we would seem fair —
One waited in whose presence we would wear,
Even as a lover who would be well-seen,
Our manhood faultless and our honor clean.

RESURGAM

Exiled afar from youth and happy love,
  If Death should ravish my fond spirit hence
I have no doubt but, like a homing dove,
  It would return to its dear residence,
And through a thousand stars find out the road
Back into earthly flesh that was its loved abode.

A MESSAGE TO AMERICA

You have the grit and the guts, I know;
You are ready to answer blow for blow
You are virile, combative, stubborn, hard,
But your honor ends with your own back-yard;
Each man intent on his private goal,
You have no feeling for the whole;
What singly none would tolerate
You let unpunished hit the state,
Unmindful that each man must share
The stain he lets his country wear,
And (what no traveller ignores)
That her good name is often yours.

You are proud in the pride that feels its might;
From your imaginary height

103

Men of another race or hue
Are men of a lesser breed to you:
The neighbor at your southern gate
You treat with the scorn that has bred his hate.
To lend a spice to your disrespect
You call him the "greaser". But reflect!
The greaser has spat on you more than once;
He has handed you multiple affronts;
He has robbed you, banished you, burned and killed;
He has gone untrounced for the blood he spilled;
He has jeering used for his bootblack's rag
The stars and stripes of the gringo's flag;
And you, in the depths of your easy-chair —
What did you do, what did you care?
Did you find the season too cold and damp
To change the counter for the camp?
Were you frightened by fevers in Mexico?
I can't imagine, but this I know —
You are impassioned vastly more
By the news of the daily baseball score
Than to hear that a dozen countrymen
Have perished somewhere in Darien,
That greasers have taken their innocent lives
And robbed their holdings and raped their wives.

 Not by rough tongues and ready fists
Can you hope to jilt in the modern lists.
The armies of a littler folk
Shall pass you under the victor's yoke,
Sobeit a nation that trains her sons
To ride their horses and point their guns —
Sobeit a people that comprehends
The limit where private pleasure ends
And where their public dues begin,
A people made strong by discipline
Who are willing to give—what you've no mind to —
And understand—what you are blind to —
The things that the individual
Must sacrifice for the good of all.

You have a leader who knows—the man
Most fit to be called American,
A prophet that once in generations
Is given to point to erring nations
Brighter ideals toward which to press
And lead them out of the wilderness.
Will you turn your back on him once again?
Will you give the tiller once more to men
Who have made your country the laughing-stock
For the older peoples to scorn and mock,
Who would make you servile, despised, and weak,
A country that turns the other cheek,
Who care not how bravely your flag may float,
Who answer an insult with a note,
Whose way is the easy way in all,
And, seeing that polished arms appal
Their marrow of milk-fed pacifist,
Would tell you menace does not exist?
Are these, in the world's great parliament,
The men you would choose to represent
Your honor, your manhood, and your pride,
And the virtues your fathers dignified?
Oh, bury them deeper than the sea
In universal obloquy;
Forget the ground where they lie, or write
For epitaph: "Too proud to fight."

I have been too long from my country's shores
To reckon what state of mind is yours,
But as for myself I know right well
I would go through fire and shot and shell
And face new perils and make my bed
In new privations, if ROOSEVELT led;
But I have given my heart and hand
To serve, in serving another land,
Ideals kept bright that with you are dim;
Here men can thrill to their country's hymn,
For the passion that wells in the Marseillaise
Is the same that fires the French these days,

And, when the flag that they love goes by,
With swelling bosom and moistened eye
They can look, for they know that it floats there still
By the might of their hands and the strength of their will,
And through perils countless and trials unknown
Its honor each man has made his own.
They wanted the war no more than you,
But they saw how the certain menace grew,
And they gave two years of their youth or three
The more to insure their liberty
When the wrath of rifles and pennoned spears
Should roll like a flood on their wrecked frontiers.
They wanted the war no more than you,
But when the dreadful summons blew
And the time to settle the quarrel came
They sprang to their guns, each man was game;
And mark if they fight not to the last
For their hearths, their altars, and their past:
Yea, fight till their veins have been bled dry
For love of the country that WILL not die.

 O friends, in your fortunate present ease
(Yet faced by the self-same facts as these),
If you would see how a race can soar
That has no love, but no fear, of war,
How each can turn from his private role
That all may act as a perfect whole,
How men can live up to the place they claim
And a nation, jealous of its good name,
Be true to its proud inheritance,
Oh, look over here and learn from FRANCE!

INTRODUCTION AND CONCLUSION OF A LONG POEM

I have gone sometimes by the gates of Death
And stood beside the cavern through whose doors
Enter the voyagers into the unseen.
From that dread threshold only, gazing back,
Have eyes in swift illumination seen

Life utterly revealed, and guessed therein
What things were vital and what things were vain.
Know then, like a vast ocean from my feet
Spreading away into the morning sky,
I saw unrolled my vanished days, and, lo,
Oblivion like a morning mist obscured
Toils, trials, ambitions, agitations, ease,
And like green isles, sun-kissed, with sweet perfume
Loading the airs blown back from that dim gulf,
Gleamed only through the all-involving haze
The hours when we have loved and been beloved.

Therefore, sweet friends, as often as by Love
You rise absorbed into the harmony
Of planets singing round magnetic suns,
Let not propriety nor prejudice
Nor the precepts of jealous age deny
What Sense so incontestably affirms;
Cling to the blessed moment and drink deep
Of the sweet cup it tends, as there alone
Were that which makes life worth the pain to live.
What is so fair as lovers in their joy
That dies in sleep, their sleep that wakes in joy?
Caressing arms are their light pillows. They
That like lost stars have wandered hitherto
Lonesome and lightless through the universe,
Now glow transfired at Nature's flaming core;
They are the centre; constellated heaven
Is the embroidered panoply spread round
Their bridal, and the music of the spheres
Rocks them in hushed epithalamium.

. . . . .

I know that there are those whose idle tongues
Blaspheme the beauty of the world that was
So wondrous and so worshipful to me.
I call them those that, in the palace where
Down perfumed halls the Sleeping Beauty lay,

Wandered without the secret or the key.
I know that there are those, of gentler heart,
Broken by grief or by deception bowed,
Who in some realm beyond the grave conceive
The bliss they found not here; but, as for me,
In the soft fibres of the tender flesh
I saw potentialities of Joy
Ten thousand lifetimes could not use. Dear Earth,
In this dark month when deep as morning dew
On thy maternal breast shall fall the blood
Of those that were thy loveliest and thy best,
If it be fate that mine shall mix with theirs,
Hear this my natural prayer, for, purified
By that Lethean agony and clad
In more resplendent powers, I ask nought else
Than reincarnate to retrace my path,
Be born again of woman, walk once more
Through Childhood's fragrant, flowery wonderland
And, entered in the golden realm of Youth,
Fare still a pilgrim toward the copious joys
I savored here yet scarce began to sip;
Yea, with the comrades that I loved so well
Resume the banquet we had scarce begun
When in the street we heard the clarion-call
And each man sprang to arms—ay, even myself
Who loved sweet Youth too truly not to share
Its pain no less than its delight. If prayers
Are to be prayed, lo, here is mine! Be this
My resurrection, this my recompense!

ODE IN MEMORY OF THE AMERICAN VOLUNTEERS FALLEN FOR FRANCE

(To have been read before the statue of Lafayette and Washington in Paris, on Decoration Day, May 30, 1916.)

I

Ay, it is fitting on this holiday,
Commemorative of our soldier dead,
When—with sweet flowers of our New England May
Hiding the lichened stones by fifty years made gray —
Their graves in every town are garlanded,
That pious tribute should be given too
To our intrepid few
Obscurely fallen here beyond the seas.
Those to preserve their country's greatness died;
But by the death of these
Something that we can look upon with pride
Has been achieved, nor wholly unreplied
Can sneerers triumph in the charge they make
That from a war where Freedom was at stake
America withheld and, daunted, stood aside.

II

Be they remembered here with each reviving spring,
Not only that in May, when life is loveliest,
Around Neuville-Saint-Vaast and the disputed crest
Of Vimy, they, superb, unfaltering,
In that fine onslaught that no fire could halt,
Parted impetuous to their first assault;
But that they brought fresh hearts and springlike too
To that high mission, and 'tis meet to strew
With twigs of lilac and spring's earliest rose
The cenotaph of those
Who in the cause that history most endears
Fell in the sunny morn and flower of their young years.

III

Yet sought they neither recompense nor praise,
Nor to be mentioned in another breath
Than their blue coated comrades whose great days
It was their pride to share—ay, share even to the death!
Nay, rather, France, to you they rendered thanks
(Seeing they came for honor, not for gain),
Who, opening to them your glorious ranks,
Gave them that grand occasion to excel,
That chance to live the life most free from stain
And that rare privilege of dying well.

IV

O friends! I know not since that war began
From which no people nobly stands aloof
If in all moments we have given proof
Of virtues that were thought American.
I know not if in all things done and said
All has been well and good,
Or if each one of us can hold his head
As proudly as he should,
Or, from the pattern of those mighty dead
Whose shades our country venerates to-day,
If we've not somewhat fallen and somewhat gone astray.
But you to whom our land's good name is dear,
If there be any here
Who wonder if her manhood be decreased,
Relaxed its sinews and its blood less red
Than that at Shiloh and Antietam shed,
Be proud of these, have joy in this at least,
And cry: "Now heaven be praised
That in that hour that most imperilled her,
Menaced her liberty who foremost raised
Europe's bright flag of freedom, some there were
Who, not unmindful of the antique debt,
Came back the generous path of Lafayette;

And when of a most formidable foe
She checked each onset, arduous to stem —
Foiled and frustrated them —
On those red fields where blow with furious blow
Was countered, whether the gigantic fray
Rolled by the Meuse or at the Bois Sabot,
Accents of ours were in the fierce melee;
And on those furthest rims of hallowed ground
Where the forlorn, the gallant charge expires,
When the slain bugler has long ceased to sound,
And on the tangled wires
The last wild rally staggers, crumbles, stops,
Withered beneath the shrapnel's iron showers: —
Now heaven be thanked, we gave a few brave drops;
Now heaven be thanked, a few brave drops were ours."

V

There, holding still, in frozen steadfastness,
Their bayonets toward the beckoning frontiers,
They lie—our comrades—lie among their peers,
Clad in the glory of fallen warriors,
Grim clusters under thorny trellises,
Dry, furthest foam upon disastrous shores,
Leaves that made last year beautiful, still strewn
Even as they fell, unchanged, beneath the changing
     moon;
And earth in her divine indifference
Rolls on, and many paltry things and mean
Prate to be heard and caper to be seen.
But they are silent, calm; their eloquence
Is that incomparable attitude;
No human presences their witness are,
But summer clouds and sunset crimson-hued,
And showers and night winds and the northern star.
Nay, even our salutations seem profane,
Opposed to their Elysian quietude;
Our salutations calling from afar,

From our ignobler plane
And undistinction of our lesser parts:
Hail, brothers, and farewell; you are twice blest, brave
    hearts.
Double your glory is who perished thus,
For you have died for France and vindicated us.

Printed in Great Britain
by Amazon